Service Innovation

This book looks at service innovation, service industries and innovation performance in services.

It seeks a broader explanation and understanding of services, service innovation and its performance, and the future of service innovation in different service industries. In addition, it discusses service domination in the big economies around the world and how that was created and supported by service innovation.

The book will be useful for academics interested in service innovation as well as practitioners in the service business.

Esam Mustafa is Professor at the Department of Management and Law at Vancouver Island University. He is also Academic Expert at the Department of Economics, Finance and Operations Management at Athabasca University. He is Chartered Manager, Operation Manager, Project Manager and Business Researcher with demonstrated working experience in the Higher Education and Management industries.

Routledge Studies in Innovation, Organizations and Technology

For more information about the series, please visit www.routledge.com/Rout-ledge-Studies-in-Innovation-Organizations-and-Technology/book-series/RIOT

Service Innovation

Esam Mustafa

Routledge
Taylor & Francis Group

LONDON AND NEW YORK

First published 2019
by Routledge
2 Park Square, Milton Park, Abingdon, Oxon OX14 4RN

and by Routledge
52 Vanderbilt Avenue, New York, NY 10017

First issued in paperback 2020

Routledge is an imprint of the Taylor & Francis Group, an informa business

British Library Cataloguing-in-Publication Data

A catalogue record for this book is available from the British Library

Library of Congress Cataloging-in-Publication Data
Names: Mustafa, Esam, author.
Title: Service innovation / by Esam Mustafa.
Description: First Edition. | New York : Routledge, 2019. | Series:
    Routledge studies in innovation, organizations and technology |
    Includes bibliographical references and index.
Identifiers: LCCN 2018057013 | ISBN 9781138314658 (hardback) |
    ISBN 9780429456817 (ebook)
Subjects: LCSH: Service industries—Technological innovations. |
    Technological innovations—Economic aspects.
Classification: LCC HD9980.5 .M87 2019 | DDC 338.4/7—dc23
LC record available at https://lccn.loc.gov/2018057013

ISBN 13: 978-0-367-67157-0 (pbk)
ISBN 13: 978-1-138-31465-8 (hbk)

Typeset in Galliard
by Apex CoVantage, LLC

to the soul of my late mother
to my father
to my love
to my family

Contents

Illustrations

Figures

Tables

Abbreviations

AIM	America Online Instant Messenger
BRIC	Brazil, Russia, India, and China
EIS	European Innovation Scoreboard
GDP	Gross Domestic Product
IoT	Internet of Things
ITO	Information Technology Outsourcing
KIBS	Knowledge Intensive Business Services
NAICS	North American Industry Classification System
NCWIT	National Center for Women in IT
NIST	National Institute of Standards and Technology
OECD	The Organization of Economic Cooperation and Development
PSS	Product-Service Systems
R&D	Research and Development
SMAC	Social, Mobile, Analytical and Cloud
SMEs	Small-and-Medium Enterprises
SNA	United Nations System of National Accounts
VR	Virtual reality

1   What is service?

Service and economies

The importance of services in national and global economies is increasing significantly. "Our welfare and the welfare of our economy now are based on services. The activities of manufacturing and agriculture always will be necessary, but we can eat only so much food and we can use only so many goods" (Fitzsimmons, Fitzsimmons, & Bordoloi, 2008).

During the last two decades, the contribution of the service sector, communication services, food services and health services to the Gross Domestic Product (GDP) has been significantly increasing in both developed and developing economies. Table 1.1 shows shares of the service sector in the GDPs of industrialized countries (United States, Japan, UK and Germany) and developing BRIC countries (Brazil, Russia, India and China).

The service sector has a huge proportion of local and global employment, too. Hence, because of its fast and continual growth, the scope and the economic potential of this sector have not yet been researched extensively (Wamboye & Nyaronga, 2018). Table 1.2 shows how the service industry has a significant impact on world employment and in selected countries with large economies, while Table 1.3 shows the overall employment contribution of the service industry in different world regions.

Table 1.1 Share of services in GDP

	% of world GDP	% share services in GDP	% share manufacturing in GDP
UK	3.9	79.94	9.76
US	27.89	78.92	12.27
Japan	5.98	70.4	20.55
China	15.09	50.24	29.78
Russia	1.86	62.65	13.77
Germany	4.59	68.88	22.81
India	2.88	52.93	16.57
Brazil	2.46	72.68	11.76

Source: The World Bank, 2018

Table 1.2 Employment in services by country (% of total employment)

Country	2007	2008	2009	2010	2011	2012	2013	2014	2015	2016	2017
World	43.93	44.69	45.43	46.23	46.95	47.73	48.45	49.22	50.07	50.74	51.09
United Kingdom	76.44	76.92	79.28	79.57	79.60	79.75	80.08	79.78	80.21	80.42	80.53
Sweden	76.07	76.53	77.67	78.02	78.08	78.33	78.81	79.42	79.68	79.91	80.00
United States	77.53	78.17	79.58	79.91	79.78	79.93	79.73	79.44	79.49	79.55	79.45
Denmark	73.53	74.36	77.12	77.97	77.71	77.70	77.99	78.26	78.21	78.82	78.63
Canada	76.40	76.68	77.68	77.90	77.88	77.89	78.00	78.36	78.56	78.54	78.43
France	73.22	74.01	74.40	74.84	74.92	75.32	75.62	76.58	76.88	76.83	76.76
Germany	67.85	68.87	69.52	70.04	70.12	70.25	70.78	70.52	70.92	71.31	71.46
Saudi Arabia	74.87	75.94	75.51	74.35	74.00	73.05	71.78	71.71	71.16	71.50	71.20
South Africa	65.11	68.57	69.68	70.74	71.22	71.72	71.50	71.93	70.56	71.09	71.07
Japan	67.50	68.48	69.53	70.22	70.53	69.94	70.06	71.10	70.46	70.88	70.93
Brazil	59.67	59.87	60.85	61.74	62.51	65.49	65.86	66.75	67.60	68.95	68.83
Russian Federation	61.82	62.41	64.11	64.51	64.86	64.91	65.28	65.76	66.11	66.34	66.42
Mexico	60.67	61.18	62.04	62.01	62.03	62.73	62.52	61.63	61.41	61.37	61.13
China	38.80	40.38	42.06	43.61	45.53	47.35	49.24	51.21	53.35	54.85	55.87
East Asia & Pacific	41.14	42.36	43.77	45.04	46.42	47.64	49.12	50.64	52.19	53.40	54.20
Turkey	49.77	49.52	51.75	50.07	49.38	50.42	50.69	51.06	52.37	53.72	53.84
Nigeria	42.92	46.44	48.70	55.28	53.58	51.68	49.92	51.16	51.78	51.86	51.81
World	43.93	44.69	45.43	46.23	46.95	47.73	48.45	49.22	50.07	50.74	51.09
Indonesia	39.90	40.44	41.23	42.19	42.82	43.00	44.07	44.32	44.92	46.46	47.11
Bangladesh	36.48	35.89	35.34	35.07	33.94	33.90	34.11	35.33	36.88	38.02	39.85
India	25.70	26.13	26.30	26.68	27.75	28.64	29.55	30.54	31.74	32.83	33.48

Source: The World Bank, 2018

Table 1.3 Employment in services by region (% of total employment)

Region	2007	2008	2009	2010	2011	2012	2013	2014	2015	2016	2017
North America	77.41	78.01	79.38	79.69	79.57	79.71	79.55	79.33	79.39	79.44	79.34
Euro area	68.27	69.29	70.45	71.14	71.56	72.03	72.60	72.85	73.03	73.25	73.30
OECD members	69.71	70.32	71.51	71.82	71.86	72.12	72.27	72.34	72.40	72.61	72.59
East Asia & Pacific	41.14	42.36	43.77	45.04	46.42	47.64	49.12	50.64	52.19	53.40	54.20
Middle East & North Africa	52.00	52.16	52.40	52.87	53.52	53.69	53.87	53.56	53.58	53.82	53.66

Source: The World Bank, 2018

Definition of service

Oxford Living dictionaries define the word "service" as "the action of helping or doing work for someone". Another definition is "[S]ervice is deeds, process and performance" (Zeithaml, Bolton et al., 2006). This definition looks to service from perspective of organizational management systems. Yet another definition of service – as an economic activity – is "Service is an economic activity that creates values and provides benefits for customers at specific times and places" (Talib, Rahman, & Qureshi, 2012). This definition looks at service from the broader theory of economics.

A service can also be defined as "a process of applying the competencies and skills of a provider for the benefit of, and in conjunction with, the customer" (Agarwal, Selen, Roos, & Green, 2015). The concept of added value has been also used to define service as "the application of resources for the benefit of another, centres on the concept of value cocreation" (Vargo & Akaka, 2012). The two definitions just presented were based on the concept of benefits and value creation between service provider and the customer. The concept of benefits and value creation is originated by the definition of service that empathizes on performance offered by a provider to a customer through economic activities aim to create value and deliver benefits at explicit time and location (Haksever & Render, 2013; Heidrich & Réthi, 2012; Lovelock & Patterson, 2015).

A definition used that refers to the intangible characteristics of service is:

> [A] service is an activity or series of activities of more or less intangible nature that normally, but not necessarily, take place in interactions between the customer and service employees and/or physical resources or goods and/or systems of the service provider, which are provided as solutions to customer problems.
>
> (Grönroos, 1990)

Classification of the service industry

Based on the literature on classifications of the service sector, there are two main trends: narrow-scope classification and broad-scope classification. Narrow service-sector classification includes all organizations that have economic activities other than manufacturing, agriculture, construction, mining, forestry, quarrying, fishing and hunting, public administration and defense, and utilities. The broad classification extends the scope of excluded industries to construction, public administration and defense, and utilities (Kanapathy, 2003).

The phrase "service industry" refers to economic activity that takes the form mainly of a personal service rather than a physical industrial commodity. This physical industrial activity is represented by a group of industries that provide goods commodities, for example, the agriculture industry, the manufacturing industry, the mining industry and the construction industry. However, the differences between industry divisions were not clear, and there were difficulties in differentiating the process of assembling goods parts from the process of serving food in a restaurant (Stigler, 1956). According to Stigler (1956) service industry classification was as follows:

- Wholesale trade
- Medical and health
- Retail trade
- Government education
- Banking and finance
- Domestic service
- Insurance and real estate
- Medical and health (private)
- Laundries, cleaning, and so on.
- Automobile repair
- Armed forces
- Hotels and lodging places
- Welfare, religious and membership organizations
- Entertainment and recreation services
- Legal, engineering and miscellaneous professional services
- Education (private)
- Business services
- Barbers and beauty shops
- Miscellaneous repair services
- Other personal services

Manufacturing industries were classified long before the service industry was, and they have historically been censused and analyzed more frequently as well. Manufacturing industries have been classified occasionally according to two classification methods: by their original raw materials and by their final developed products. Examples of the classification method used with respect to raw material are wood, oil and rubber products. Examples of the classification method used with respect to final developed products are cars and machines. However, the classification methods keep changing because they are usually technology-based classifications, and technology changes quickly.

However, using the same classification methods in the service industries would result in unpractical classification, because services do not generally end by creating physical products. Therefore, service industry classification methods started by following occupational structure (Stigler, 1956). According to the occupational structure, services industries include:

- Food
- Medical care
- Clothing
- Education
- Automobiles

- Trade
- Household operation (domestic servants)
- Entertainment and recreation
- Household furnishing
- Community welfare and religious
- Personal care
- Fuel, light and refrigeration
- Insurance
- Miscellaneous personal services
- Non-profit membership
- Government

The North American Industry Classification System (NAICS), Canada 2017 version, classifies service industries into 15 subcategories:

- Wholesale trade
- Retail trade
- Transportation and warehousing
- Information and cultural industries
- Finance and insurance
- Real estate and rental and leasing
- Professional, scientific and technical services
- Management of companies and enterprises
- Administrative and support, waste management and remediation services
- Educational services
- Health care and social assistance
- Arts, entertainment and recreation
- Accommodation and food services
- Other services (except public administration)
- Public administration

Wholesale trade industry

NAICS defines the wholesale industry in this way: "This sector comprises establishments primarily engaged in wholesaling merchandise, generally without transformation, and rendering services incidental to the sale of merchandise".

Under this sector there are two main types of wholesalers: merchant wholesalers and brokers. The merchant wholesalers sell and buy merchandise for their own accounts and possess the goods they sell. They usually have their own locations, offices and warehouse. They deal with suppliers or they have their own shipping system and autos to operate from their warehouse to their distribution centers and customer locations. They also usually have additional businesses such as marketing and support services, logistics services, packaging, labeling, handling of warranty claims, inventory management, shipping and product training. Examples of merchant wholesalers are wholesale distributors, drop shippers and import-export merchants. Sales branches or offices, excluding retailers, used by manufacturing, refining, or mining organizations for showing and marketing their products are considered merchant wholesalers. Additionally, merchant wholesalers include units that do not own the input materials and that completely outsource the process of developing and producing goods.

Brokers includes business-to-business electronic markets and agents. Brokers arrange for the operations of purchasing or selling of goods owned by other parties, usually for an agreed fee. Their other names are import-export agents, commission merchants, manufacturer's representatives and auction companies. They generally operate from their own offices.

More detailed wholesale sector subsectors are as follows:

- Farm product merchant wholesalers
- Petroleum and petroleum products merchant wholesalers
- Food, beverage and tobacco merchant wholesalers
- Personal and household goods merchant wholesalers
- Motor vehicle and motor vehicle parts and accessories merchant wholesalers
- Building material and supplies merchant wholesalers
- Machinery, equipment and supplies merchant wholesalers
- Miscellaneous merchant wholesalers
- Business-to-business electronic markets, and agents and brokers

Retail trade

This sector includes establishments primarily involved in retailing and selling merchandise that usually needs no transformation. Since retailing is the last step of distributing goods, retailing deals with relatively small quantities of goods. This sector has two sub-retailer types, store and non-store retailers.

Store retailers

Store retailers have fixed locations that try to attract large numbers of customers. In general, this kind of retail store has a wide range of displayed merchandise. Examples of retail stores are gasoline stations, electrical equipment and tools supplies stores, and building materials stores. In addition to selling and offering merchandise, retail stores provide sales associate services like repairing and installation services.

Non-store retailers

Non-store retailers have different retailing methods compared to retailing stores. They offer to customers merchandise using methods like information broadcasting, door-to-door marketing, electronic catalogues, in-home demonstration, vending machines and temporary displays. This type of retail also includes businesses that do home delivery, offering such services as newspaper delivery.

Subsectors of the retail trade sector are as follows:

- Furniture and home furnishings stores
- Health and personal care stores
- Electronics and appliance stores
- Building material and garden equipment and supplies dealers
- Gasoline stations
- Food and beverage stores
- Clothing and clothing accessories stores
- Sporting goods, hobby, book and music stores
- General merchandise stores
- Miscellaneous store retailers
- Non-store retailers

Transportation and warehousing

This sector includes businesses that provide passenger transportation, transportation of goods, and warehousing and storing of goods. Transportation uses air, water, road, rail and pipeline. Warehousing and storage businesses are classified based on the type of facilities and services. Further detailed subsectors under this sector are:

- Rail transportation
- Water transportation
- Truck transportation
- Transit and ground passenger transportation
- Pipeline transportation
- Scenic and sightseeing transportation
- Support activities for transportation
- Postal service
- Couriers and messengers
- Warehousing and storage

Information and cultural industries

The information and cultural sector includes businesses that produce and distribute information and culture-related products. Their activity includes providing access to equipment, data processing and transmitting products. However, the real consideration in classifying this sector is the intangible services and intangible products they provide, not the goods or the materials. Further detailed subsectors under this sector are:

- Telecommunications
- Motion picture and sound recording industries
- Publishing industries

- Broadcasting (except Internet)
- Data processing, hosting and related services
- Other information services

Finance and insurance

The finance and insurance service sector includes businesses that provide or facilitate financial transactions and services related to the formation, liquidation or transfer of ownership of financial assets. Financial transactions in this sector are of two kinds: financial intermediation and underwriting annuities and insurance. Financial intermediation is dealing with deposits, issuing securities, making loans and purchasing securities, while underwriting annuities and insurance services involves collecting insurance fees, building up reserves, investing those reserves and making contractual payments. Further detailed subsectors of this sector are:

- Monetary authorities – central bank
- Credit intermediation and related activities
- Securities, commodity contracts and other financial investment and related activities
- Insurance carriers and related activities
- Funds and other financial vehicles

Real estate and rental and leasing

This sector includes businesses that provide renting, leasing, selling, appraising or allowing the use of assets services, and has three subsectors:

- Real estate
- Rental and leasing services
- Lessors of non-financial intangible assets (except copyrighted works)

Professional, scientific and technical services

This sector includes businesses that provide services in which people are the main input. Those business institutions usually sell expertise through providing knowledge and skills. The subsectors under this sector are:

- Engineering and related services
- Legal services accounting
- Bookkeeping and payroll services
- Tax preparation
- Computer systems design and related services
- Architectural
- Specialized design services
- Scientific and technical consulting services

- Management
- Public relations
- Scientific research and development services
- Advertising

However, educational establishments whose main activity is delivering a wide variety of training and instruction in many subjects and those establishments whose main activity is providing health care services are not included in this sector.

Management of companies and enterprises

The management of companies and enterprises sector includes businesses whose main activity is managing companies and enterprises. This includes those businesses whose activity is managing and holding financial assets and securities of companies and enterprises with which they hold a controlling interest.

Administrative and support, waste management and remediation services

This sector includes businesses whose main activity is supporting day-to-day operations of other companies and those business whose main activity is managing waste activities of other companies.

Supporting such day-to-day operations includes hiring and placing employees and workers, doing the daily administration tasks, preparing documents, collecting payments for claims, taking orders from customers, managing and arranging travel, cleaning buildings, providing security and surveillance, and packaging and labeling products of other companies. Waste management businesses are those that collect and dispose of waste, operate facilities of material recovery, clean septic tanks and deal with polluted places.

Educational services

This sector includes businesses whose main activity is providing a wide variety of instruction and training. Universities, colleges, schools and training centers are all included in this sector. In addition, they may also offer accommodation and services to their students. All businesses in the sector usually follow the same process and have teachers' with expertise in their subjects and the required teaching ability.

Health care and social assistance

This sector includes businesses whose main activity is providing health care services, including diagnosis and treatment, and that provide residential care services for medical or social reasons. In addition, these businesses provide counseling, community housing and food services, welfare services, child protection and vocational rehabilitation and child care. The main subsectors included under this sector are:

- Ambulatory health care services
- Hospitals
- Nursing and residential care facilities
- Social assistance

Arts, entertainment and recreation

This sector includes businesses whose main activity is operating facilities, providing cultural services and providing entertainment and recreational services. Activities in this sector include producing and promoting live performances, participating in live performances, producing events for public viewing; providing artistic expositions, providing for the display of artistic products, providing skills of live performances, operating sports facilities, providing sport recreational activities and leisure services.

The main subsectors included under this sector are:

- Performing arts, spectator sports and related industries
- Heritage institutions
- Amusement, gambling and recreation industries

Accommodation and food services

This sector includes businesses whose main activity is providing short-term hospitality services to customers. In this sector, hotels, resorts, motor hotels, motels, casino hotels, bed and breakfast accommodations, recreational vehicle parks and campgrounds, housekeeping cottages and cabins, and hunting and fishing camps are included. The main subsectors included under this sector are Accommodation services and Food services and drinking services places.

Public administration

This sector includes establishments whose activities are of a governmental nature. Activities such as taxation, judicial interpretation of laws and regulations, legislative activities, national defense activities, foreign affairs and international activities, public order and safety services, immigration services and the administration of government-related programs.

The main subsectors included under this sector are:

- Federal government public administration
- Provincial and territorial public administration
- Local, municipal and regional public administration

- Aboriginal public administration
- International and other extraterritorial public administration

Other services

This sector includes all establishments that are not classified to any other service sectors. It includes those establishments whose activities are repairing, providing general routine machinery maintenance for ensuring work efficiently, laundry services, providing funeral services, providing pet care services, providing photo finishing services, organizing and conducting religious activities, and supporting social and political causes and endorsing and defending the interests of their members.

The main subsectors included under this sector are:

- Repair and maintenance
- Personal and laundry services
- Religious, grant-making, civic and professional and similar organizations
- Private households

Categories of services

The earlier service classification frameworks have classified services based on goods marketing perspectives. One of the earlier service classification frameworks is to categorize services based on goods ownership to three types services: owned goods service, rented goods service and non- goods services (Judd, 1964). Owned goods service is the services of creating, improving or repairing a product. Rented goods service is the right to use or own a product, while non-goods service is experimental possession. Like Judd's classification framework, Rathmell (1974) categorized services based on type of buyers, type of sellers, motives of buyers and practices of buyers.

A different classification model considers the level of intangibility that is involved with services or goods-based services (Shostack, 1977). There are many companies that are not goods or production companies. These services companies are usually not marketed in the same way as goods are marketed due to the lack of success of using the goods production marketing models. For example, hospitality and banking services would not succeed when marketed using the same marketing model used for marking automobiles. Thus, considering the level of intangibility of the services is important to classify them under goods services or away from that.

Another different service classification framework argues to apply deeper insights into services. The framework call to go beyond the goods-based services classification and investigate the characteristics of the service itself. Examples of these characteristics are the nature of service itself, the relationship between the service organization and the customers, the level of customization, the demand and the supply of the service, and the service delivery method (Lovelock, 1983).

Another classification model categorizes four main groups to define the service sector. The categorization was based on two measurements (Schmenner, 1986). The first measurement concerns how the service developed and was delivered (is it by devices involvement or by human factor involvement?), whereas the second measurement concerns the level of service customization and the level of relationship between suppliers and customers. Schmenner's four categories are Professional Service, Service Factory, Service Shop and Mass Service (Heidrich & Réthi, 2012).

Professional service

In the professional services category, labor-intensity and customization have the same level of importance in creating and delivering the service. Therefore, this type of service is sometimes known as mutual services. Health care and healing services provided by doctors is one example of professional services. Doctors cannot provide their services unless there is someone or some people asking for it because of sickness, health welfare or life improvement. A doctor creates his/her specific service according to the specific customer's need. Other examples are legal consultation service, representation service provided by a law consultant or a lawyer, architecture service, business consultation service and education and training. All these services are provided to individuals and organizations to solve their simple and complex issues and problems. The main characteristic of professional services is the high contact between service provider and the customer. Hence customers have high participation in creating the service. High customer participation has its effect on the level of service quality and on the level of cost of the service and delivery process.

Service factory

The main characteristic of this type of service is the low customization and low interaction. There is no intensive labor work involved in creating and delivering the service. Instead of labor-intensity, equipment and machines are involved more in the services process and costs. Therefore, standardization is important in such a service, which leads to low customization. Examples of this type of service are logistics services, hospitality services and fast food restaurants.

Service shop

The main characteristic in this type of service is the higher interaction between customers and service providers compared to the service factory type. Therefore, customizations and addressing customers' needs are more important and follow relatively low standardization. Examples of this type are automobile repair services and health care in hospitals.

Mass service

The main characteristic of mass service is that it is very labor-intensive and low on customization and interaction. This type of service usually follows a level of standardization which leads to low interaction between service providers and customers. Examples of mass service are wholesale and retail trade service and banking services.

Zeithaml, Bitner, and Gremler (2006) categorized services into four groups: service industries, derived service, intangible products and customer service. Service industries are the companies with service as their main product, such as hotels and transportation companies. The intangible product is the unphysical products such as training services and consulting services. Derived services are the services from physical products such as computers that provide data processing services. Customer service is the supporting services for products such as maintenance services and setting up machines (Talib et al., 2012).

The Organization of Economic Cooperation and Development (OECD) categorized services industry into four main categories: goods services such as logistics services, information services such as call centers, knowledge-based services such as financial services and people services such as health care services (Directorate for Science Technology and Industry STI, 2008).

Servitizing the industry

There is an increased concern about how to integrate services in goods industries. This increased concern emerged because of the increased transformation from goods and production to service business (Baines, Lightfoot, Benedettini, & Kay, 2009). Value attracts customers and develops a sense of the services and goods. Hence, creating successful and effective values usually accompanies profit and revenue. In addition, transforming the focus from goods to goods-based services increases goods marketing, offerings, promotions and revenue. Examples of services bundled with good selling are long-term and short-term warranties, free maintenance offers and time-based discounts revenue. The evolution of goods-based services leads to the Product-Service Systems (PSS) for increasing sales and achieving more revenue.

The use of PSS is called servitization. Servitization is a method of opening new ways for more revenue. Based on PSS, servitization is an innovative way to help organizations to create values through transforming their business to selling PSS (Ennis, Barnett, De Cesare, Lander, & Pilkington, 2018; Pistoni & Songini, 2017).

Since the idea of servitization means mainly the goods-related services, it has to make a difference to that good's value and offering otherwise servitization would not be useful. It has to add a significant value to the goods that it was created with. The significant improvement is the value that is brought by servitization (Pistoni & Songini, 2017). By doing so, servitization transforms the business of goods to a new business paradigm with significant new values, costs and revenue.

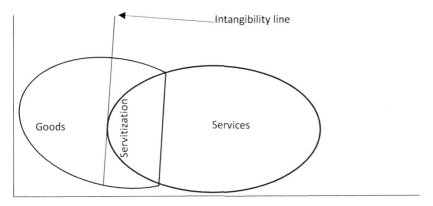

Figure 1.1 Servitization
Source: author

Servitization turns services into an effective strategy, and they have become a main distinguishing factor of a business's offering. This is the reason manufacturing companies transform their offering strategy from pure goods to goods and services bundles.

Servitization combines the focus on goods and the focus on products. In other words, servitization models are framing service, with all its characteristics of intangibility, into good products to create or increase the value of that good. Shown in Figure 1.1, when the line of intangibility moves toward the good, it indicates a high level of servitization; when it moves toward services, it indicates a low level of servitization, and if it moves completely to the services, servitization vanishes.

References

Agarwal, R., Selen, W., Roos, G., & Green, R. (2015). *The handbook of service innovation*. Springer.

Baines, T. S., Lightfoot, H. W., Benedettini, O., & Kay, J. M. (2009). The servitization of manufacturing: A review of literature and reflection on future challenges. *Journal of Manufacturing Technology Management, 20*(5), 547–567.

R&D and innovation in services. (2008). *Directorate for Science Technology and Industry*. Organisation for Economic Co-operation and Development. Retrieved from http://www.oecd.org/dataoecd/44/55/49995531.pdf

Ennis, C., Barnett, N., De Cesare, S., Lander, R., & Pilkington, A. (2018). A conceptual framework for servitization in industry 4.0: Distilling directions for future research. *Proceeding of the Advance Services Group Spring Servitization Conference 2018*. Aston University and Higher Education Academy. Retrieved from https://westminsterresearch.westminster.ac.uk/download/eb9d44c826b2505adbf-778c6525b004b5e5d30a82b0544518fd877465064ef3a/127252/Ennis%20et%20al%20A%20conceptual%20framework%20for%20servitization%20in%20Industry%204.0%20Servitization%20Conference%20%20Amends10Apr2018.pdf

Fitzsimmons, J. A., Fitzsimmons, M. J., & Bordoloi, S. (2008). *Service management: Operations, strategy, and information technology.* New York, NY: McGraw-Hill.

Grönroos, C. (1990). *Service management and marketing: Managing the moments of truth in service competition.* Jossey-Bass.

Haksever, C., & Render, B. (2013). *Service management: An integrated approach to supply chain management and operations.* FT Press.

Heidrich, B., & Réthi, G. (2012). Services and service management. In *Service science research, strategy and innovation: Dynamic knowledge management methods* (pp. 1–36). IGI Global.

Judd, R. C. (1964). The case for redefining services. *Journal of Marketing, 28*(1), 58–59.

Kanapathy, V. (2003). Services sector development in Malaysia: Education and health as alternate sources of growth. In *AT120 Research Conference* (pp. 20–21). Numora Foundation. Retrieved from https://www.nomurafoundation.or.jp/en/wordpress/wp-content/uploads/2014/09/20030220-21_Vijayakumari_Kanapathy.pdf

Lovelock, C. (1983). Classifying services to gain strategic marketing insights. *The Journal of Marketing,* 9–20.

Lovelock, C., & Patterson, P. (2015). *Services marketing.* Pearson Australia.

Pistoni, A., & Songini, L. (2017). The servitization of manufacturing: Why and how. In *Servitization Strategy and Managerial Control* (Vol. 32, pp. 1–5). Emerald Publishing Limited. https://doi.org/doi:10.1108/S1479-351220170000032001

Rathmell, J. M. (1974). *Marketing in the service sector.* Cambridge, MA: Winthrop Publishers

Schmenner, R. W. (1986). How can service businesses survive and prosper. *Sloan Management Review, 27*(3), 21–32.

Shostack, G. L. (1977). Breaking free from product marketing. *The Journal of Marketing,* 73–80.

Stigler, G. (1956). *Trends in employment in the service industries.* Princeton University Press.

Talib, F., Rahman, Z., & Qureshi, M. N. (2012). Total quality management in service sector: A literature review. *International Journal of Business Innovation and Research, 6*(3), 259–301.

Vargo, S. L., & Akaka, M. A. (2012). Value cocreation and service systems (re) formation: A service ecosystems view. *Service Science, 4*(3), 207–217.

Wamboye, E. F., & Nyaronga, P. J. (2018). *The Service Sector and Economic Development in Africa.* Routledge.

The World Bank. (2018). *World development indicators.* Retrieved from http://databank.worldbank.org/data/reports.aspx?source=2&type=metadata&series=SL.IND.EMPL.ZS#

Zeithaml, V. A., Bitner, M. J., & Gremler, D. D. (2006). *Services marketing: Integrating customer focus across the firm* (4th ed.). Singapore: Mc-Graw Hill.

Zeithaml, V. A., Bolton, R. N., Deighton, J., Keiningham, T. L., Lemon, K. N., & Petersen, J. A. (2006). Forward-looking focus: Can firms have adaptive foresight? *Journal of Service Research, 9*(2), 168–183. https://doi.org/10.1177/1094670506293731

2 What is innovation?

Definition of innovation

The concept of innovation, especially innovation in service, is still facing many arguments and contradicted thoughts. For example, the technological innovation concept and meaning challenge the concept of service concepts with regard to the type of product, uniqueness of service, intangibility characteristic of service and the use of technology (Gallouj & Djellal, 2011). The arguments and the different thoughts emerge from the impact of different management theories and management cultures on the process of innovation.

Scholars have worked their efforts towards a collective definition for innovation and created a general innovation theory. An example of these efforts is the systems theory approach. It provides a common theoretical basis to describe innovation as changes (Read, 2000). Similar to this view, innovation was defined as unique new ideas that are implemented to make changes (Ven, 2017).

Baregheh, Rowley, and Sambrook (2009) defined innovation as "multi-stage process whereby organizations transform ideas into new/improved products, service or processes, in order to advance, compete, and differentiate themselves successfully in their marketplaces".

A similar approach is the definition by the Organization for Economic Co-operation and Development (OECD, 2008): "[I]nnovation is the implementation of a new or significantly improved product (good or service), or process, a new marketing method, or a new organizational method in business practices, workplace organization or external relations". The OECD definition incorporated the previous definitions given for Daft & Becker and Damanpour (1978; 1988).

Another definition of innovation is that by Crossn & Apaydin (2010). They defined innovation as production or adoption, assimilation and exploitation of a value-added novelty in economic and social spheres; renewal and enlargement of products, services and markets; development of new methods of production; and establishment of new management systems. It is both a process and an outcome.

One definition similar to Crossan & Apaydin's in viewing innovation as wholistic managerial level considers managers and employees. This definition considers innovation as the planned and introduced ideas, processes, procedures or products within the role of an organization and new to the applicable unit of adoption, designed significantly to benefit the groups, individuals, the organization or wider society (West & Farr, 1990). This definition enriches innovation to be more than just financial return. It focuses on the significance of innovation. Therefore, this definition does not include the minor changes in the process. It is important for innovation to be new to the unit of adoption. That means innovation does not have to be new to the society and world but just new to the organization (Wihlman, 2014; Hartley, 2014; Fuglsang & Pedersen, 2011).

Theories of innovation

There is no overall theory of innovation so far. That is because innovation thinking has involved many frameworks of thought. In most of the thinking framework, innovation is viewed as a activity more complex than it looks. However, one consistent theme found in the organization management literature is that its research and analysis results have been inconsistent (Read, 2000; Wolfe, 1994). The inconsistency in innovation research theories is because of the variety of researchers' interests. Researchers are from various fields, and sometimes they focus on a specific type or category of innovation, in a specific type or category of organizations, and focus on different dimensions of innovation. Therefore, it is believed that coming up with a general theory of innovation is difficult (Read, 2000).

The economist Joseph Schumpeter (1883–1950) is the first person to be mentioned when talking about innovation. He analyzed the dominant capitalist economic model and developed a theory that the ability of firms to innovate was related to the size of the firm. He claimed that the flexibility of small firms makes them more innovative than large firms which might get trapped in an embedded structure. One important view in his theory is the "creative destruction" concept. This concept calls for restructuring the market to innovate faster. However, Schumpeter's theory has no strong empirical evidence to demonstrate the relationship between firm size and its ability to innovate.

Kline and Rosenberg (1986) developed the chain-linked innovation model. The model characterizes the innovation process from a technical activities point of view, involves the external competition of markets and considers the complexity of the relationships and interactions among innovation process stages (Léger & Swaminathan, 2007).

As Schumpeter's theory lacks any empirical support, academics continued investigating innovation topics, and many theories emerged. Abernathy & Utterback (1978) developed a theoretical differentiation between incremental innovation and radical innovation. Porter (1986) demonstrated a similar concept based on discontinuous and continuous technological changes. Incremental-Breakthrough innovation contrast is also presented by Tushman and Anderson (1986).

Abernathy and Utterback (1978) developed an innovation model consisting of the interaction of organizational structure, product innovation, process innovation and environment. The model was developed through three main phases. The fluid phase is the first phase, which consists of implementing great changes.

The second phase is the traditional phase, which involves focusing on technological application and customer needs to start growing in the market. In the third phase, the company becomes mature in innovation and starts to focus on specific customers, driven by market segmentation and trends.

Henderson and Clark (1990) argue, through a new model, that the incremental-radical innovations contrast model is not sufficient to clarify how organizations can be innovative. Henderson and Clark's model, based on "knowledge of the components and knowledge of the linkage between them" and called the "architectural knowledge" model, classified innovation into four types: architectural, radical, incremental and modular (Henderson & Clark, 1990).

Christensen (1997) noticed that some radical innovation supported the existing position of incremental innovation in some industries which opposed the predication of some innovation models such as Henderson-Clark's. After investigating innovation in the hard drive industry, he developed the Disruptive Innovation Theory. The theory has classified innovation into two types: staining innovation and disruptive innovation. He argues that part of "innovators' dilemma" is that they "overshoot" customers' needs and market demand. This means that innovators develop technologies and products that customers may not need. Sustaining innovation is a kind of innovation that is likely to be more incremental, while disruptive innovation is radical in nature.

Disruptive innovation is also characterized by the fact that it is not produced and presented according to customers' needs. Such innovation when compared with existing products is simpler, cheaper and of lower quality. In the early phase, disruptive innovations will achieve the marginal targeted goal or will open new markets for the company. Over time, disruptive innovation products improve faster with the increase of customer demand compared to the existing sustaining innovation product.

Types of innovation

Crossan and Apaydin (2010) argue that innovation types should be understood through two main types: (1) innovation as a process for creating ideas and properly implementing them, and (2) innovation as outcomes which are the end results of implementation. The process is the manner and techniques by which an idea is created and implemented, while outcomes are the products, services or business processes that result. Understanding and knowing innovation types are essential for organizations. Hurmelinna-Laukkanen, Sainio, and Jauhiainen (2008) argue that each type of innovation needs a specific treatment and response from the organization.

Typology of innovation varies between studies. However, there are two typology approaches that are dominant: technological innovation versus administrative innovation and radical innovation versus incremental innovation (Zhao, 2005). In addition to these two dominant typology approaches, many scholars used product and process innovation typology to refer to the technological innovation.

Technological innovation versus administrative innovation

Technological innovation is the adoption of new technologies that are incorporated into processes or products (Damanpour, 1988). Technological innovation provides long-term success in markets through high competitive advantages (Grover, Purvis, & Segars, 2007). Administrative innovation refers to the implementation of new ideas to improve organizational processes, routines, structures or systems (Elenkov, Judge, & Wright, 2005). There are two types of innovations under technological innovation: product innovation and process innovation. Product innovation is creating a new good or service to improve on existing goods or services (Burgelman, Wheelwright, & Christensen, 2009). Process innovation, on the other hand, focus on improving the effectiveness and efficiencies of production (Tarafdar & Gordon, 2007).

Administrative innovation is associated with internal processes supporting the delivery of a service or product. In some studies, administrative innovation refers to an organizational innovation, and in other studies it refers to management innovation. Tables 2.1, 2.2 and 2.3 provide examples of the definitions suggested by different studies.

Radical innovation versus incremental innovation

Radical innovations are new and different than previous innovations, while incremental innovations alter existing innovations (Golder, Shacham, & Mitra, 2009). To be radical, innovations must be unique and novel. The most radical innovations are the ones that are new to the world and are exceptionally different from existing innovations. An example of a radical innovation is AOL's instant messenger (AIM) service. AOL was the first to start a contemporary Internet-wide messenger service in May 1997. Another example is Amazon, which stated selling

Table 2.1 Definitions of management innovation

Scholar	Definition
(Kimberly & Evanisko, 1981)	Any program, product or technique which represents a significant departure from the state of the art of management at the time it first appears, and which affects the nature, location, quality or quantity of information that is available in the decision-making process
(Hamel, 2006)	A marked departure from traditional management principles, processes and practices or a departure from customary organizational forms that significantly alters the way the work of management is performed
(Birkinshaw & Mol, 2006)	The generation and implementation of a management practice, process, structure or technique that is new to the state of the art and is intended to further organizational goals

Table 2.2 Definitions of organizational innovation

Scholar	Definition
(Edquist, Hommen, & McKelvey, 2001)	New ways to organize business activities such as production or R&D, and innovations that have to do with the organization of human resources
OECD (2005)	"A new or significantly improved knowledge management system implemented to better use or exchange information, knowledge and skills within the firm" and/ or "a major change to the organization of work within the firm, such as change in the management structure or the integration of different departments or activities" and/or "a new or significant change in the firm's relationships with other firms or public institutions, such as through alliances, partnerships, outsourcing or sub-contracting"
Damanpour (1988)	Innovative change in a non, or rather less, technological manner to a firm's nature, structure, arrangement, practices, beliefs, rules or norms

Table 2.3 Definitions of administrative innovation

Scholar	Definition
Abernathy and Utterback (1978); Daft and Becker (1978)	New approaches and practices to motivate and reward organizational members, devise strategy and structure of tasks and units, and modify the organization's management processes
(Tanninen, Jantunen, & Saksa, 2008)	Innovations that are related to management activities and are connected with the organization's social system
(Ahire & Ravichandran, 2001)	Embody the adoption of administrative programs, processes or techniques new to the adopting organization
Damanpour (1988)	Innovations that occur in the social system of an organization, including rules, roles, procedures and structures related to the communication and exchange among people and between the environment and people
Daft and Becker (1978)	Pertains to the policies of recruitment, allocation of resources and the structuring of tasks, authority and reward, and is related to the administrative core of the organization

books online, enabling it to offer numerous numbers of books compared to traditional book stores. An example in technology is the transistor created by Bell Labs, which played a major role in the electronics industry.

Incremental innovations, on the other hand, involve revisions or alterations to existing products or service (Burgelman et al.,2009). This addition improves business processes that achieve and increase customer satisfaction. Examples of incremental innovations are the video and audio messengers that allow seeing and talking with another person or group concurrently. Another example is the continuous increase in computers' processing rates.

OECD's innovation typology

The *Oslo Manual of OECD* (*OECD*)differentiates between four main types of innovations: product, process, organizational and marketing innovation. *OECD* defined each type of innovation as shown in Table 2.4.

Open innovation

Open innovation is "a distributed innovation process based on purposively managed knowledge flows across organizational boundaries" (Bogers, Chesbrough, & Moedas, 2018). Open innovation comes from ideas from inside or outside an organization. It can be deployed from inside or outside too. The open innovation model can be viewed as the reverse of the traditional innovation model, where research and development (R&D) brings innovations and ideas from within the organizations. Therefore, the difference is that open innovation uses internal and external knowledge to boost internal innovation and create markets for the newly innovated goods and services. Open innovation is a model that considers organizations' need to use both external ideas and internal ideas to reach the market. In other words, open innovation includes internal and external ideas in the same model (Bogers et al., 2018; Chesbrough, Vanhaverbeke, & West, 2006). Hence, open innovation assumes that ideas generated from inside an organization can be taken to the market through external paths to be enriched, enhanced and

Table 2.4 OECD's innovation types

Innovation	*Definition*
Product innovation	The introduction of a good or service that is new or significantly improved with respect to its characteristics or intended uses. This includes significant improvements in technical specifications, components and materials, incorporated software, user friendliness or other functional characteristics.
Process innovation	The implementation of a new or significantly improved production or delivery method. This includes significant changes in techniques, equipment and/or software.
Organizational innovation	The implementation of a new organizational method in the firm's business practices, workplace organization or external relations.
Marketing innovation	The implementation of a new marketing method involving significant changes in product design or packaging, product placement, product promotion or pricing.

Source: OECD, 2005

evaluated. Based on this concept, open innovation values outside-organizations' ideas and always tries to reach out to the knowledge outside the organization.

The difference between open innovation and closed (previous) innovation

Innovation has been extensively studied during recent decades, and there are many different types described and used in the literature (Abernathy & Utterback, 1978; Bon & Mustafa, 2013; Christensen, 1997). Over the years, organizational innovation has been studied to optimize, improve and figure out new ways to turn ideas into profitable products and services (Grover et al., 2007; Thomas, 2018). Before open innovation emerged, the closed innovation methods and models dominated the internal R&D units in industrial production organizations. Open innovation began to emerge when closed innovation was challenged by continuous improvement issues that hindered coming up with new methods to sustain or create competitive advantage in the expanding international market. The role of R&D was mainly an internal one intended for new products and services or a role intended to improve existing ones. The internal R&D units were challenged by the extensive external knowledge that could open different channels to the market.

The first difference between open innovation and closed innovation is the increase of using and employing external knowledge. In closed innovation, external knowledge is used less and is considered as an additional tool that used when needed. It is not integrated into the process of innovation in the way internal knowledge was. Employing more external knowledge decreases the use of the internal R&D unit. Using external knowledge focuses on the external ideas that enrich the thinking about the innovation and helps in coming up with new services and products, opening new markets, developing new departments and enhancing internal and external innovation-related relationships.

The second difference is the scope of the innovation subject in the organization. Open innovation moves innovation thinking to accept any idea that occurs while searching external knowledge. An organization that tries to find a solution or to come up with improvements to apply to specific subject problems may come across many ideas when looking into external resources. These emerging ideas can change the innovation thinking and the need within that organization, while in closed innovation, thinking and searching may be limited to the specific first subject only (Bogers et al., 2018; Chesbrough et al., 2006). For example, Amazon initially was an online bookstore, but when it opened to new external market ideas, it turned into an online enterprise that sells many products and services (Quinn, 2015; see Amazon time line in Table 2.5).

The third difference is related to the technical measurement of innovation. The earlier innovation frameworks did not consider the any type of measurement error when analyzing and evaluating their R&D research and outcomes (Chesbrough et al., 2006). Open innovation helps organizations to go to market through different and diversified channels with no restrictions or R&D results-based directions.

Table 2.5 Amazon's open innovation time line

1995	Amazon launched as an online book retailer
1997	Amazon reached $438m capital
1998	Amazon started to sell CDs and DVDs
1999	Amazon started to sell electronics
2000	Amazon expanded to be a third-party business
2001	Amazon acquired Borders.com
2002	Amazon web service launched
2003	Amazon started to sell jewelry
2004	Amazon started to sell shoes
2005	Amazon launched Prime membership
2006	Amazon started to sell fresh food
2007	Amazon launched Kindle e-reader
2008	Amazon games launched
2010	Amazon studios launched
2011	Amazon Kindle Fire launched
2012	Amazon acquired Kiva robotic company
2013	Amazon Art launched
2014	Amazon Echo launched
2015	Amazon market capital reached $245bn
2016	Amazon Drone-based delivery launched
2017	Amazon acquires Whole Food store
2018	Amazon opens cashier-less grocery store

Source: Quinn (2015); *The Telegraph*

Innovation measurements

More than a few studies, such as that of Prasad and Nori (2008), measured and evaluated innovation. Organization innovation is measured through percentage of profit or sale resulting from the innovation initiatives; rate of new products, service or solutions provided; number of ideas generated; number of patent submissions; total cumulative working hours set into an innovation initiative and variety of human resource capital (Hage, 1999).

Measuring innovation in service should be based on performance indicators of the firm (Voss, 1992). Voss listed the following indicators: financial improvement, development achieved comparing with the competition, useful employment of resource, flexibility of the process, degree of service quality, effectiveness of the innovation, speed of implementation and cost of the innovation process and program.

Another measurement innovation model, excerpted from European Innovation Scoreboard (EIS), is used for measuring innovation in service. Kanerva and Hollanders's model included the following: business R&D expenditures, non-R&D innovation expenditures, collaborating with others, level of firm renewal, resource efficiency innovators, average of share of innovation, new-to-market sales, new-to-firm sales, employment in innovation, knowledge-intensive services and knowledge-intensive services exports (Kanerva & Hollanders, 2009).

The most important elements that influence innovation are the characteristics of top managers and staff. In addition, other elements have notable influence on innovation and its outcomes, such as organizational culture that supports innovation, availability of business resources, general political environment, social atmosphere and technical settings (Gambatese & Hallowell, 2011).

Some scholars have reported that the capacity of an organization for innovation has significantly influenced different factors: the ability to deal with conflicts in the organization (Hausman, 2005), industry experience (Damanpour & Schneider, 2006), gender factors (Sonfield, Lussier, Corman, & McKinney, 2001), age of top managers and senior staff (Huber & Glick, 1993), level of education of managers (Hausman, 2005) and willingness to share responsibility and control (Gambatese & Hallowell, 2011).

References

Abernathy, W., & Utterback, J. (1978). Patterns of industrial innovation. *Technology Review*, *80*(7), 40–47.

Ahire, S. L., & Ravichandran, T. (2001). An innovation diffusion model of TQM implementation. *IEEE Transactions on Engineering Management*, *18*(4), 445–464.

Baregheh, A., Rowley, J., & Sambrook, S. (2009). Towards a multidisciplinary definition of innovation. *Management Decision*, *47*(8), 1323–1339. https://doi.org/10.1108/00251740910984578

Birkinshaw, J., & Mol, M. (2006). How management innovation happens. *MIT Sloan Management Review*, *47*(4), 81–88.

Bogers, M., Chesbrough, H., & Moedas, C. (2018). Open innovation: Research, practices, and policies. *California Management Review*, *60*(2), 5–16. https://doi.org/10.1177/0008125617745086

Bon, A. T., & Mustafa, E. M. A. (2013). Impact of total quality management on innovation in service organizations: Literature review and new conceptual framework. *Procedia Engineering*, *53*, 516–529. https://doi.org/http://dx.doi.org/10.1016/j.proeng.2013.02.067

Burgelman, R. A., Wheelwright, S. C., & Christensen, C. M. (2009). *Strategic management of technology and innovation*. New York, NY: McGraw-Hill.

Chesbrough, H., Vanhaverbeke, W., & West, J. (2006). *Open innovation : Researching a new paradigm*. Oxford: Oxford University Press. Retrieved from http://ebookcentral.proquest.com/lib/viu/detail.action?docID=430378

Christensen, C. (1997). *The innovator's dilemma : When new technologies cause great firms to fail*. Boston: Harvard Business School Press.

Crossan, M. M., & Apaydin, M. (2010). A multi-dimensional framework of organizational innovation: A systematic review of the literature. *Journal of Management Studies*, *47*(6), 1154–1191. https://doi.org/10.1111/j.1467-6486.2009.00880.x

Daft, R., & Becker, S. (1978). *Innovation in organizations: Innovation adoption in school organizations*. New York: Elsevier.

Damanpour, F. (1988). Innovation type, radicalness and the adoption process. *Communication Research*, *15*(5), 545–567. https://doi.org/doi: 10.1177/009365088015005003

Damanpour, F., & Schneider, M. (2006). Phases of the adoption of innovation in organizations: Effects of environment, organization and top managers1. *British Journal of Management*, *17*(3), 215–236. https://doi.org/10.1111/j.1467-8551.2006.00498.x

Edquist, C., Hommen, L., & McKelvey, M. (2001). *Innovation and Employment: Process versus Product Innovation.* Cheltenham: Edward Elgar Publishing.

Elenkov, D. S., Judge, W., & Wright, P. (2005). Strategic leadership and executive innovation influence: An international multi-cluster comparative study. *Strategic Management Journal, 26*(7), 665–682. https://doi.org/10.1002/smj.469

Fuglsang, L., & Pedersen, J. S. (2011). How common is public sector innovation and how similar is it to private sector innovation? In *Innovation in the public sector* (pp. 44–60). Springer.

Gambatese, J. A., & Hallowell, M. (2011). Factors that influence the development and diffusion of technical innovations in the construction industry. *Construction Management and Economics, 29*(5), 507–517. https://doi.org/10.1080/01446 193.2011.570355

Golder, P. N., Shacham, R., & Mitra, D. (2009). Findings: Innovations' origins: When, by Whom, and how are radical innovations developed? *Marketing Science, 28*(1), 166–179. https://doi.org/10.1287/mksc.1080.0384

Grover, V., Purvis, R. L., & Segars, A. H. (2007). Exploring ambidextrous innovation tendencies in the adoption of telecommunications technologies. *Engineering Management, IEEE Transactions On, 54*(2), 268–285. https://doi.org/10.1109/tem.2007.893995

Hage, J. (1999). Organizational innovation and organizational change. *Annual Review of Sociology, 25*, 597–622.

Hamel, G. (2006). The why, what, and how of management innovation. *Harvard Business Review, 84*(2), 72–84.

Hartley, J. (2014). New development: Eight and a half propositions to stimulate frugal innovation. *Public Money & Management, 34*(3), 227–232.

Hausman, A. (2005). Innovativeness among small businesses: Theory and propositions for future research. *Industrial Marketing Management, 34*(8), 773–782. https://doi.org/10.1016/j.indmarman.2004.12.009

Henderson, R. M., & Clark, K. B. (1990). Architectural innovation: The reconfiguration of existing product technologies and the failure of established firms. *Administrative Science Quarterly, 35*(1), 9–30.

Huber, G. P., & Glick, W. H. (1993). *Organizational change and redesign: Ideas and insights for improving performance.* New York: Oxford University Press.

Hurmelinna-Laukkanen, P., Sainio, L. M., & Jauhiainen, T. (2008). Appropriability regime for radical and incremental innovations. *R&D Management, 38*(3), 278–289.

OECD. (2005). Oslo Manual. *Guidelines for Collecting and Interpreting Innovation Data.* Paris: OECD Publication. Retrieved from http://www.sourceoecd.org/scienceIT/9264013083

Kanerva, M., & Hollanders, H. (2009). *The impact of the economic crisis on innovation: Analysis based on the innobarometer 2009 survey.* Maastricht: Directorate for Enterprise and Industry, European Commission. Retrieved from www.merit.unu.edu/about/profile.php?id=647&stage=2

Kimberly, J., & Evanisko, M. (1981). Organizational innovation: The influence of individual, organizational, and contextual factors on hospital adoption of technological and administrative innovations. *Academy of Management Journal, 24*(4), 689–713.

Léger, A., & Swaminathan, S. (2007). *Innovation theories: Relevance and implications for developing country innovation* (DIW Discussion Papers No. 743). Berlin. Retrieved from http://hdl.handle.net/10419/27267

Porter, M. E. (1986). *Competition in global industries.* Harvard Business Press.

Prasad, V., & Nori, K. (2008). Systems approach for adoption of innovations in organizations. *Systemic Practice and Action Research, 21*(4), 283–297. https://doi.org/10.1007/s11213-008-9097-5

Quinn, J. (2015). Amazon timeline: From internet bookshop to the world's biggest online retailer. *The Telegraph.* Retrieved from www.telegraph.co.uk/technology/amazon/11801515/Amazon-timeline-from-internet-bookshop-to-the-worlds-biggest-online-retailer.html.

Read, A. (2000). Determinants of successful organisational innovation: A review of current research. *Journal of Management Practice, 3*(1), 95–119.

Sonfield, M., Lussier, R., Corman, J., & McKinney, M. (2001). Gender comparisons in strategic decision-making: An empirical analysis of the entrepreneurial strategy matrix. *Journal of Small Business Management, 39*(2), 165–173. https://doi.org/10.1111/1540-627x.00015

Tanninen, K., Jantunen, A., & Saksa, J. M. (2008). Adoption of administrative innovation within organization: An empirical study of tqm metamorphosis. *International Journal of Innovation and Technology Management, 05*(03), 321–340. https://doi.org/10.1142/S0219877008001412

Tarafdar, M., & Gordon, S. R. (2007). Understanding the influence of information systems competencies on process innovation: A resource-based view. *Journal of Strategic Information Systems, 16*(4), 353–392. https://doi.org/10.1016/j.jsis.2007.09.001

Therrien, P., Doloreux, D., & Chamberlin, T. (2011). Innovation novelty and (commercial) performance in the service sector: A Canadian firm-level analysis. *Technovation, 31*(12), 655–665. https://doi.org/10.1016/j.technovation.2011.07.007

Thomas, E. (2018). From closed to open innovation in emerging economies: Evidence from the chemical industry in Brazil. *Technology Innovation Management Review, 8*(3). Retrieved from http://timreview.ca/article/1144

Tushman, M. L., & Anderson, P. (1986). Technological discontinuities and organizational environments. *Administrative Science Quarterly,* 439–465.

Van De Ven, A. H. (2017). The innovation journey : You can 't control it, but you can learn to maneuver it. *Innovation, 9338*(May), 1–4. https://doi.org/10.1080/14479338.2016.1256780

Voss, C. A. (1992). Measurement of INNOVATION and design performance IN SERVICES. *Design Management Journal (Former Series), 3*(1), 40–46. https://doi.org/10.1111/j.1948-7169.1992.tb00586.x

West, M. A., & Farr, J. L. (Eds.). (1990). Innovation and creativity at work: Psychological and organizational strategies. In *Innovation and creativity at work: Psychological and organizational strategies.* Oxford, England: John Wiley & Sons.

Wihlman, T. (2014). *Innovation in municipal welfare services.* Mälardalen University.

Wolfe, R. A. (1994). Organizational innovation: Review, critique and suggested research directions. *Journal of Management Studies, 31*(3), 405–431.

Zhao, F. (2005). Exploring the synergy between entrepreneurship and innovation. *International Journal of Entrepreneurial Behaviour & Research, 11*(1), 25–41. https://doi.org/10.1108/13552550510580825

3 Innovation in service

Definition of service innovation

Service innovation is "new developments in activities undertaken to deliver core service products for various reasons" (Oke, 2007). Service innovation is recombining diverse resources in new or different ways to come up with added value (Witell et al., 2017). Another way of thinking about service innovations views them as a combination of many resources that together create value or solve a problem (Barrett, Davidson, Prabhu, & Vargo, 2015; Vargo & Akaka, 2012).

Scholars also think of service as single principle and describe service innovation as the effect of a transformation in service process. The transformation may occur in a new process, such as a new service development, new service promotion, new service delivery or a change in a process needed to enhance, synchronize and extend the connection between providers and customers (Küpper, 2001; Mustafa & Bon, 2012). This view resulted from studies focused on viewing services independently from goods (Ettlie & Rosenthal, 2012).

Research conducted to understand service innovation shows the development of three different stages over time, with each stage having different perspectives (Carlborg, Kindström, & Kowalkowski, 2014). The structure of these three stages also indicates specific forms of service innovation.

The first evolutionary stage emerged from services marketing and expanded quickly as a subject of service research in the productions and industrial marketing research domain (Carlborg et al., 2014; Gustafsson, Kristensson, Schirr, & Witell, 2016). Early services marketing research was exploratory and took risks, seeing perceived marketing as a traditional activity focused on goods instead of services. This also describes the stage of service innovation research that emerged with difficulty in the middle of a complete focus on product-centric technological innovation research that was developed by Research and Development (R&D).

Following the extensive focus on production and process-centered innovation, a new trend started to frame the need for paying attention to service innovation theories and application. This new trend followed the demarcation research view that opposed the previous assimilation view. The focus shifted to the development of the innovative service. Specifically, the focus was changed to study services offering and – how to develop successful services in the market. That change followed by arguments call for treating services apart from products and developing services innovation frameworks independently from goods and products. The arguments of treating services independently from goods products have developed a new research scope focused on the unique characteristics of services.

Terms such as intangibility, heterogeneity and low level of tradability have started to be common in the literature and service research (Atuahene-Gima, Slater, & Olson, 2005; de Brentani, 2001; Macaulay et al., 2010; Miles, 2008). The newly emerged service innovation research in this earlier stage was challenged by the prevailing view of technology-based innovation, which focused on the process and the production of goods and was supported by the prevailing production innovation theories (Abernathy & Utterback, 1978; Utterback & Abernathy, 1975).

In this stage, scholars and researchers focused on robust methods of demarcation. Some of them were the first group of scholars to establish the area of service innovation research not linked to the prevailing goods-centered innovation research (Gallouj, Fa'iz, & Weinstein, 1997; Gallouj & Djellal, 2011; Gallouj & Savona, 2009). The work of Gallouj and the coauthors have developed service research based on service characteristics that differentiate services from goods. They framed services innovation frameworks not typically following the prevailed approach of technological and non-technological paradox of innovation.

Service innovation differs from goods innovation because of the unique characteristics of service and service operations (Rubalcaba, 2012; Miles, 2008). Service innovation can be in terms of a multidimensional framework consisting of three dimensions of classification. The three dimensions are: service-based innovations activities, organizational units that are linked to service innovation and service innovations in service organizations (Rubalcaba, 2012).

As service innovation was not a well-established area of research, there was an apparent need to demonstrate the particularity of service innovation compared to product innovation and to use demarcation as the main logical approach (Atuahene-Gima et al., 2005; de Brentani, 2001). The most significant insight evolving from the research during this stage was the argument for supporting the call for developing new perspectives of the service innovation research field based on the specific characteristics of services (Yasin, Alavi, Kunt, & Zimmerer, 2004). As a result, researchers have developed grounds for service innovation research that depend on theories and models different from those for production and product-centered innovation research. Those early scholars started the first stage of the evolution of service innovation and brought attention to the unique characteristics of services to develop new service research perspectives.

The second stage was in the beginning of the current century (Carlborg et al., 2014). Marketing research has started to get intensively interested in customers' roles and participants in the service innovation and service process. Customer involvement also started to receive significantly more attention as a service innovation topic. In this stage, the new research perspective focuses on specific services, such as the process of dealing with customer interaction with the service provider, customer involvement in the service innovation creation, customer roles in service delivery and customer satisfaction with services. However, the focus was on the role of customers in the innovation process. During this stage, a great interest in service innovation was developed. This great interest resulted from the increase in scholarly work on the new service research approach (Ettlie & Rosenthal, 2011; Küpper, 2001). During this stage, new service research topics started to be explored and studied, including the deeper details of how customer involvement influences service process. The emerging results from the extensive studies emphasized the importance of staying connected with customers to know their satisfaction and their future intention with the service they brought. Topics raised during this phase involved how organizations can be successful in their service innovation activities and what factors might help increase an organization's service innovation performance.

Based on the new trends of focusing on service innovation separately from goods manufacturing innovation, the paradigm of innovation has started to get a different perspective by including new arguments on new types of innovation. Innovation types added service innovation and linked them to organizational innovation, market innovation, administrative innovation and managerial innovation. Therefore, innovation researchers extended their interest to involve the main management topics from organizational behavior, human resources, organizational studies, and leadership and strategy. The interest was on what the relationships are between those topics and services innovation and the role of technology in service innovation (Van Riel, Lemmink, & Ouwersloot, 2004).

As a result of all the increased interest in service innovation, customer involvement in services and the broader roles of management topics on service innovation, the service innovation paradigm started to change to adapt a synthesis approach (Carlborg et al., 2014). A possible justification for this change is that perceptions from demarcation researchers were consistent with the new insights of studying service innovation in manufacturing and technology innovation services (Gallouj & Savona, 2009). This includes the new studies that focused on the telecommunication technologies booming in the beginning of this century.

In this stage there was a focus also on the source of the value in the product-based services. The critical issues were to figure out what contributes to value creation for the customer. Is it the original product or is it the added services linked to that product? In addition, there were many other critical questions placed in this stage to determine which innovation type is applicable to services – is it the technological or the non-technological type (Morrar, 2014)? This argument leads to questioning the relationship between goods innovation and services innovation in the paradigm of the synthesis approach that calls for integrative studies.

The third stage in service innovation evolution was characterized with a multidimensional approach (Carlborg et al., 2014; Karniouchina, Victorino, & Verma, 2006). The new perspectives of service innovation in this stage included more complex topics in service innovation. Topics like the effect of focusing on customer satisfaction on service innovation performance, the long-term results of customer focus strategies and their effect on organizational survival in the market and dealing with the relationship between services innovation and rapid technological changes started to take place in most of the service innovation scholarly work (Den Hertog, Van der Aa, & De Jong, 2010; Gago & Rubalcaba, 2007; Rubalcaba, 2012).

As a result, many scholars argued redefining service innovation is important in order to include the new research findings that considered service innovation as separate concept from product-based concept (Fuglsang, Sundbo, & Sørensen, 2011; Witell et al., 2016). Hence, a new definition of service innovation has emerged, and that led to new views on the integrative approach of relationships between service innovation and goods innovation, extending scope of research to address more how and why questions on service innovation. That led to increase the thinking of service innovation in the real business practices rather that theoretical insights.

The emergence of service-dominant logic has impacted service innovation, service process in manufacturing and the service delivery process. Service-dominant logic is the process of applying capabilities through goods and services that involve the whole organizational unit (Fitzsimmons, Fitzsimmons, & Bordoloi, 2008).

During this stage, service innovation received increased focus among both service organizations and manufacturing organizations as a resource for achieving competitive advantages and performance excellence (Grönroos, 2007). Many scholars focused on service innovation revenue as the main measure or criterion to test the impact of services innovation on organizational performance. In addition, service innovation process deployment and service delivery have received increased interest. In this, studies on the aspect of service delivery that integrated with the service innovation process have been noted by many scholars (Chen, Li, & Chu, 2011; O'Cass, Song, & Yuan, 2013).

The evolution of service innovation research

Innovation in service organizations has become a chief issue in today's economic research and practice. That is due to the economic transition from product-based innovation to a service-support and solutions focus (Bitner & Brown, 2008; Chae, 2012; Fitzsimmons et al., 2008). The importance of innovation in service is increased because of the increase of services in international and local economic activities. Thus, investigating service innovation areas is important in determining organizational performance (Chae, 2012; Oke, 2007). The earlier emergence of service innovation was explained by the growing importance of service in the manufacturing industry, which is called by the term servitization (Santamaría, Jesús Nieto, & Miles, 2012; Vandermerwe & Rada, 1988) and service product (Miles, 2008). Such terms were emphasized in the significance of service in manufacturing industries.

Service innovation strategies

One of the significant service innovation moves was focusing on customer satisfaction. The strategy of service innovation involving customer relations was part of the findings of Scupola and Nicolajsen (2010). Their findings indicated that customers can be the path to achieving success in service innovation in service organizations. Scupola and Nicolajsen argue that customers can be a good source of service innovation ideas which can be observed from customer feedback, through tracking customer behavior when they use the electronic services or even from their complaints.

Cheng and Krumwiede (2012) concluded that an inter-functional coordination strategy has a positive influence on performance of radical service innovation. They drew their conclusion from analyzing data collected to investigate the relationship between service innovation and market orientation. Their additional analysis showed that competitor orientation has an impact on new service performance with an intermediary role of radical service innovation. Furthermore, Cheng and Krumwiede's finding also indicated a positive relationship between customer focus and incremental service innovation.

Grawe, Chen, and Daugherty (2009) conducted a study on service innovation aimed to find out how service innovation relates to strategic orientation. Their results indicated that there is a positive relationship between service innovation and the market as well as between service innovation and customer focus.

Service innovation strategy was also studied by Nunta, Ooncharoen, and Jadesadalug (2012), but from a different perspective. Nunta and colleagues' analysis results indicated a positive role of service innovation strategy on business performance in service companies. Service innovation strategies addressed are the attitude toward change, the innovative idea and the productive learning. Business performance is illustrated through the image of the corporate, excellence of service, competitive proficiency and market opportunities.

In contrast to the findings of Grawe et al. (2009) and Nunta et al. (2012), Palmer and Griswold (2011) found that the direct relationship between service innovation and a company's competitive strategy in small service firms may not always exist. In other words, small services firms are likely to engage in innovation simply to follow competitors. In this case, the initiative is a competitive response initiative rather than an innovation initiative. The study, however, did not underestimate the importance of an external competition environment and competitor orientation in services innovations.

To achieve higher sales from service innovations, firms need to enter a market earlier to present their newest service innovations. This strategy was a part of findings of a study conducted by Therrien, Doloreux, and Chamberlin (2011). Therrien and colleagues further argue that the importance of entering a market earlier may vary between firms but is still a success strategy, especially with regard to the extensive competitive market.

Sebastiani and Paiola (2010) identified four strategy paths that lead to success service innovation. All those strategies were identified as non-technology pathways that lead to service innovation and its success. The suggested paths consist of enriching and conceptualizing the offers, employing information and communication technology systems effectively, duplicating models of the company's business and diversifying market targets. Sebastiani and Paiola (2010) argue that those four strategic paths are the common paths followed by most of the companies that achieve service innovation success. Their further analysis also showed that any of the four paths gives the expected success. However, framing the four paths in one system model and implementing them would result in significant optimized outcomes.

Another study having the same approach as Sebastiani and Paiola was conducted by Chen, Li, and Chu (2011). Chen and his colleagues found three factors that have a significant impact on the success of service innovations. The factors consist of management of customer relationship, improved operation performance and accessibility of resources. Chen and colleagues analyzed data collected from mobile video service companies to identify the factors that may influence service innovation success and to find out the degree of service innovation in those companies.

Another service innovation strategy path is suggested by Lightfoot and Gebauer (2011). Their suggested path asserts that aligning determinants and strategies of service innovation will lead to successful service innovation implementation and higher innovation outcomes. For instance, fitting high-quality, strong technical skills with a service quality strategy leads to successful service innovation. Another instance, fitting product functionality with a customer focus strategy leads to service marketing and sales innovation.

References

Abernathy, W., & Utterback, J. (1978). Patterns of industrial innovation. *Technology Review*, *80*(7), 40–47.

Atuahene-Gima, K., Slater, S. F., & Olson, E. M. (2005). The contingent value of responsive and proactive market orientations for new product program performance*. *Journal of Product Innovation Management*, *22*(6), 464–482. https://doi.org/10.1111/j.1540-5885.2005.00144.x

Barrett, M., Davidson, E., Prabhu, J., & Vargo, S. L. (2015). Service innovation in the digital age: Key contributions and future directions. *MIS Quarterly*, *39*(1), 135–154.

Birkinshaw, J., & Mol, M. (2006). How management innovation happens. *MIT Sloan Management Review*, *47*(4), 81–88.

Bitner, M. J., & Brown, S. W. (2008). The service imperative. *Business Horizons, 51*, 39–46. Retrieved from http://wpcarey.asu.edu/csl/upload/The-Service-Imperative-Bitner-and-Brown-6-07-submission.pdf

Carlborg, P., Kindström, D., & Kowalkowski, C. (2014). The evolution of service innovation research: A critical review and synthesis. *The Service Industries Journal*, *34*(5), 373–398. https://doi.org/10.1080/02642069.2013.780044

Chae, B. (2012). An evolutionary framework for service innovation: Insights of complexity theory for service science. *International Journal of Production Economics*, *135*(2), 813–822. https://doi.org/10.1016/j.ijpe.2011.10.015

Chen, R., Li, Z., & Chu, C. H. (2011). Toward service innovation: An investigation of the business potential of mobile video services in China. *Journal of Technology Management in China*, 6(3), 216–231. https://doi.org/10.1108/17468771111157436

Cheng, C. C., & Krumwiede, D. (2012). The role of service innovation in the market orientation: New service performance linkage. *Technovation*, 32(7–8), 487–497. https://doi.org/10.1016/j.technovation.2012.03.006

de Brentani, U. (2001). Innovative versus incremental new business services: Different keys for achieving success. *Journal of Product Innovation Management*, 18(3), 169–187. https://doi.org/10.1016/s0737-6782(01)00071-6

Den Hertog, P., Van der Aa, W., & De Jong, M. W. (2010). Capabilities for managing service innovation: Towards a conceptual framework. *Journal of Service Management*, 21(4), 490–514.

Ettlie, J. E., & Rosenthal, S. R. (2011). Service versus manufacturing innovation. *Journal of Product Innovation Management*, 28(2), 285–299. https://doi.org/10.1111/j.1540-5885.2011.00797.x

Ettlie, J. E., & Rosenthal, S. R. (2012). Service innovation in manufacturing. *Journal of Service Management*, 23(3), 440–454. https://doi.org/10.1108/09564231211248499

Fitzsimmons, J. A., Fitzsimmons, M. J., & Bordoloi, S. (2008). *Service management: Operations, strategy, and information technology*. New York, NY: McGraw-Hill.

Fuglsang, L., Sundbo, J., & Sørensen, F. (2011). Dynamics of experience service innovation: Innovation as a guided activity: Results from a Danish survey. *The Service Industries Journal*, 31(5), 661–677. https://doi.org/10.1080/02642060902822109

Gago, D., & Rubalcaba, L. (2007). Innovation and ICT in service firms: Towards a multidimensional approach for impact assessment. *Journal of Evolutionary Economics*, 17(1), 25–44. https://doi.org/10.1007/s00191-006-0030-8

Gallouj, F., & Djellal, F. (2011). *The handbook of innovation and services: A multidisciplinary perspective*. Cheltenham: Edward Elgar Publishing.

Gallouj, F., & Savona, M. (2009). Innovation in services: A review of the debate and a research agenda. *Journal of Evolutionary Economics*, 19(2), 149–172. https://doi.org/10.1007/s00191-008-0126-4

Gallouj, F., & Weinstein, O. (1997). Innovation in services. *Research Policy*, 26(4–5), 537–556.

Grawe, S. J., Chen, H., & Daugherty, P. J. (2009). The relationship between strategic orientation, service innovation, and performance. *International Journal of Physical Distribution & Logistics Management*, 39(4), 282–300. https://doi.org/10.1108/09600030910962249

Grönroos, C. (2007). *Service management and marketing: Customer management in service competition*. Oxford, England: John Wiley & Sons.

Gustafsson, A., Kristensson, P., Schirr, G. R., & Witell, L. (2016). *Service innovation*. Business Expert Press.

Karniouchina, E. V, Victorino, L., & Verma, R. (2006). Product and service innovation: Ideas for future cross-disciplinary research. *Journal of Product Innovation Management*, 23(3), 274–280.

Küpper, C. (2001). Service innovation – A review of the state of the art. *Munich Business Administration*, 6/2001(September), 1–46.

Lightfoot, H. W., & Gebauer, H. (2011). Exploring the alignment between service strategy and service innovation. *Journal of Service Management*, 22(5), 664–683. https://doi.org/10.1108/09564231111175004

Macaulay, L., Miles, I., Wilby, J., Tan, Y. L., Theodoulidis, B., & Zhao, L. (2010). *Case studies in service innovation*. Manchester: Centre for Service Research, Manchester Business School.

Miles, I. (2008). Patterns of innovation in service industries. *IBM Systems Journal*, 47(1), 115–128. https://doi.org/10.1147/sj.471.0115

Morrar, R. (2014). Innovation in services: A literature review. *Technology Innovation Management Review*, (April), 6–14. Retrieved from www.timreview.ca

Mustafa, E., & Bon, A. (2012). Optimizing service innovation through strategies: A review. In *international conference on global optimization and its applications (ICoGOIA 2012)*. Bandung: Padjadjaran University.

Nunta, S., Ooncharoen, N., & Jadesadalug, V. (2012). The effects of service innovation strategy on business performance of spa business in Thailand. *International Journal of Business Research*, 12(3), 35–55. Retrieved from http://search.ebscohost.com/login.aspx?direct=true&db=bth&AN=77478231&site=ehost-live

O'Cass, A., Song, M., & Yuan, L. (2013). Anatomy of service innovation: Introduction to the special issue. *Journal of Business Research*, 66(8), 1060–1062. https://doi.org/10.1016/j.jbusres.2012.03.002

Oke, A. (2007). Innovation types and innovation management practices in service companies. *International Journal of Operations & Production Management*, 27(6), 564–587.

Palmer, J., & Griswold, M. (2011). Product and service innovation within small firms: An exploratory case analysis of firms in the restaurant industry. *International Journal of Business & Social Science*, 2(13), 221–223. Retrieved from http://content.ebscohost.com/ContentServer.asp?T=P&P=AN&K=64758569&S=R&D=bth&EbscoContent=dGJyMNLe80SeqLM4v+bwOLCmr0uep69Ssau4S7KWxWXS&ContentCustomer=dGJyMPGnr0uvqbNIuePfgeyx44Dt6fIA%5Cnhttp://search.ebscohost.com/login.aspx?direct=true&db=bth&AN=64758569&

Rubalcaba, L. (2012). Shaping, organizing, and rethinking service innovation: A multidimensional framework. *Journal of Service Management*, 23(5), 696–715. https://doi.org/10.1108/09564231211269847

Santamaría, L., Jesús Nieto, M., & Miles, I. (2012). Service innovation in manufacturing firms: Evidence from Spain. *Technovation*, 32(2), 144–155. https://doi.org/10.1016/j.technovation.2011.08.006

Scupola, A., & Nicolajsen, H. W. (2010). Service innovation in academic libraries: Is there a place for the customers? *Library Management*, 31(4/5), 304–318. https://doi.org/10.1108/01435121011046362

Sebastiani, R., & Paiola, M. (2010). Rethinking service innovation: Four pathways to evolution. *International Journal of Quality and Service Sciences*, 2(1), 79–94. https://doi.org/10.1108/17566691011026612

Therrien, P., Doloreux, D., & Chamberlin, T. (2011). Innovation novelty and (commercial) performance in the service sector: A Canadian firm-level analysis. *Technovation*, 31(12), 655–665. https://doi.org/10.1016/j.technovation.2011.07.007

Utterback, J. M., & Abernathy, W. J. (1975). A dynamic model of process and product innovation. *Omega*, 3(6), 639–656. https://doi.org/10.1016/0305-0483(75)90068-7

Vandermerwe, S., & Rada, J. (1988). Servitization of business: Adding value by adding services. *European Management Journal*, 6(4), 314–324. https://doi.org/10.1016/0263-2373(88)90033-3

Van Riel, A. C. R., Lemmink, J., & Ouwersloot, H. (2004). High-technology service innovation success: A decision-making perspective. *Journal of Product Innovation Management*, 21(5), 348–359.

Vargo, S. L., & Akaka, M. A. (2012). Value co-creation and service systems (re) formation: A service ecosystems view. *Service Science*, *4*(3), 207–217.

Witell, L., Gebauer, H., Jaakkola, E., Hammedi, W., Patricio, L., & Perks, H. (2017). A bricolage perspective on service innovation. *Journal of Business Research*, *79*, 290–298. https://doi.org/https://doi.org/10.1016/j.jbusres.2017.03.021

Witell, L., Snyder, H., Gustafsson, A., Fombelle, P., & Kristensson, P. (2016). Defining service innovation: A review and synthesis. *Journal of Business Research*, *69*(8), 2863–2872. https://doi.org/https://doi.org/10.1016/j.jbusres.2015.12.055

Yasin, M. M., Alavi, J., Kunt, M., & Zimmerer, T. W. (2004). TQM practices in service organizations: An exploratory study into the implementation, outcome and effectiveness. *Managing Service Quality*, *14*(5), 377–389. https://doi.org/10.1108/09604520410557985

4 Service innovation performance

Service innovation among countries

The capability to innovate is explained as the attitude towards exploiting and taking advantage of new ideas successfully. It is also described as an internal energy for generating and exploring new ideas, for experimenting with solutions, for finding the potential opportunity in the market and for developing these opportunities as marketable and effective innovations. Innovation capability is also defined as the ability to generate and create new knowledge for regenerating the value of the business. Some studies highlighted the fact that innovation capability has a multidimensional nature and has independencies among its components. According to the system perspective of innovation capabilities, the concept of capability to innovate consists of seven interdependent elements: organizational structure, a system for interfacing with the mainstream organization, a mechanism for exploring processes, developing the skills and talent for the organization, governance within the organization, a mechanism for decision-making, suitable culture and leadership (Gil-Garcia, Helbig, & Ojo, 2014).

The United Nations System of National Accounts (SNA) has defined the term services as "the result of any production activity which facilitates the consumption of consuming products" The services are facilitating the following processes:

1 Services includes the transportation, cleaning, altering or repairing the already produced consumer goods.
2 Services facilitate the changes in the physical condition of the people, providing them accommodation, transport facilities, medical treatments, improving their appearances, and so on.
3 Services can also change the mental condition of the people, by providing services in terms of education, entertainment, advice and information.

The definition of services explains that service plays vital role in the development of the country. Different research studies have indicated that the growing role of services in developed economies has accounted for almost 70% of the GDP of the country. The development of services in developing countries is considered to be the major source for productivity growth. In developed and developing economies such as the United States, India, China, Brazil, Canada and Germany, service innovation has occurred throughout the economy. Extended globalization and economic crises around the globe have revealed the importance of service-based R&D and innovation for growth of the firms and industries in these countries. The significance of service innovation is well defined in today's global world. Many firms are finding new ways to develop the type of service innovation in order to survive in global competition (Carlborg, Kindström, & Kowalkowski, 2014). Also, there should be appropriate policy recommendations by international organizations like OECD for improving service innovation in its member countries, such as the United States, India, China, Brazil, Canada and Germany.

Service innovation and its characteristics

Service innovation is explained as the merger of product innovation and process innovation. Product innovation is known as the development of a new product or having qualitative changes in existing products, whereas process innovation is the introduction of a new process for developing or delivering goods and services. Innovation in services is marked by service concepts, delivery systems in service sector, client interfaces and technologies, and also includes the ways in which the customers view and use a specific service (Lusch & Nambisan, 2015).

The service sector is comprised of approximately 70% of the employment of OECD countries. The services are not only important for service sector but are widely spread in other sectors such as manufacturing. The economies of developed and developing countries are now becoming service-oriented, and distinctions between services and non-services are diminishing. The services are becoming significant for the employment performance of the economy of a country. This is also evident from the number of employment opportunities from this sector, although in developed countries the services are labor-intensive as compared to manufacturing industries. Therefore, matching supply with demand is more challenging in service industries than in manufacturing industries. It is estimated that service activities are expected to increase in importance, as there is growth from demand side and the response of the supply side is vital and essential. Moreover, the service sector is innovating with globalization in the world. Innovation in the service sector is significant for competition and performing well. Innovation is considered to be the key for service performance.

Management challenges of service innovation

The development of innovation capabilities is strongly associated with the strategic intention of the business to be innovative, that is, the desired strategy for innovation. Two major challenges associated with innovation hinder the development of innovation capability. The first challenge is how to raise managers' awareness about the importance of innovation. The second challenge is related to the promotion of organizational commitment towards the need for innovation and developing the innovation capability. When the organizations are moving towards their maturity stage, the most difficult capabilities to change are those related to processes and values, both significant components of innovation capabilities.

Some of the other challenges associated with innovation management are described as follows:

- What to change? Even when the organization is sure about the need for innovation, they may find difficulties in developing an appropriate innovation agenda. Innovation can be in different forms, ranging from simple innovation to incremental development. Innovation can range from changes in what is offered by the organization, that is, its products or services to how the offered products are developed and delivered to the users. The innovation also reflects the positioning of an offering. Therefore, it is challenging for the business to what form of innovation should be adopted by the organization.

- Understanding the innovation: The problem of managing innovation is the way people think about it. For example, sometimes there is considerable confusion about the invention and innovation. Reforming thinking about innovation is about developing new insights to open new possibilities and recognizing market needs that have not been met yet.

- Continuous learning: The agenda of innovation is constantly shifting, and it is required that organizations should develop routines to deal with the key challenges that emerge from their environment. There is plenty of scope for organizations to learn and adapt to these routines. Therefore, to remain innovative in the market the organizations needs to have continuous learning. The difference in adopting and innovation is that when one is blindly copying, it is adopting, whereas in innovation it is adopting and developing a good practice which other organizations are using.

- Dealing with discontinuity: Innovation is usually considered as a "steady state" activity. Of course, the innovation is about the change, but it takes place within a system which is relatively consistent. Therefore, the organizations have to develop the business environment where innovation is not discontinuous but is a continual process.

The above-mentioned challenges are general to all business around the world. Some of the specific challenges for countries in the OECD for businesses seeking to accelerate innovation are:

- Access to capital funding
- Access to entrepreneurial skills
- Limited access to international markets
- A risk of adverse culture

Around the globe there are regions where the ability to innovate is concentrated. These regions are in developed countries such as the United States, Europe, Canada and Japan. However, this situation is now changing as emerging markets like China and India are making a transition from production capabilities to innovative capabilities not only in service but also in their manufacturing industry (Rodionova & Epifantseva, 2017).

Service innovation in Brazil

Likewise, in Brazil, systematic efforts for innovation in service are emerging. To keep innovating, the Brazilian companies are carrying out internal and external efforts. Internal efforts are enhancing internal R&D, training of employees for developing their skills to use innovative techniques, using financial resources for developing and enhancing the ability to deal with change. External efforts include use of new technology, acquiring patents and licenses, acquisition of software program and so on (Moser, de Oliveira, & Bueno, 2017).

Research studies have been conducted in Brazil on different institutes, government agencies, private firms and so on in order to understand innovation. These studies have shown that innovation is increasingly a significant topic for researchers, government institutes and the private sector. One of the studies shows that executives in private businesses are clear that innovation is a significant factor for remaining competitive in the business. Some of the businesses in Brazil lack the roots of innovation in their process, and few of them have adopted a structured process of innovation (Lopes & Barbosa, 2014).

For stimulating service innovation in the country, the government of Brazil has developed a national policy related to innovation in science, technology and innovation. The objective of the government is to develop the private sector as a contributor to the economic and social development of Brazil. Therefore, this will be a contribution to all the entire Brazilian society.

Different laws and regulations in Brazil encourage the development of innovation in the country. The Technological Innovation Act (2004) was developed in order to facilitate the development of a specialized and cooperative environment for innovation. This law has also encouraged scientific and technological institutions to participate in service innovation in the service sector. The government of Brazil has promoted creation of investment funds for innovation (Lopes & Barbosa, 2014).

As compared to other regions, Brazil is the last among the emerging countries which is concentrating on innovation in the production and service sectors. According to the latest data collected from the Ministry of Science, Technology and Innovations and Communications (MCTIC), in 2013, only 1.6% of total GDP of the country was spent on innovation and technology in different sectors of the country. It was estimated that 1.6% of GDP is almost R$85.6 billion, from which R$63.7 billion was invested in Research and Development (R&D). The private sector in Brazil had R$ 26.5 billion of investment.

In 2014, the National Institute of Industrial Property (INPI) received almost 4,000 patent applications. MCTIC data revealed in 2014 that around 35% of the companies in Brazil have already implemented product and process innovation. This is an ideal situation in which innovations help organizations achieve sustainable advantages based on organizational resources, capabilities and skills.

Service innovation in India

India is a country full of different societies, religions, people and cultures. It has a great variety of customers for its business organizations. Owing to its demographic factors, business organizations keep on working to capture the market, to retain the customer, to earn additional profit by formulating innovative policies and by constructing models related to services. Organizations are competing on the basis of services and by providing personalized services to their customers.

Service innovation has been a vital part of the business world and plays a great role in creating the value proposition of products and enhancing any competitive edge in the market in recent years. There are different types of businesses – some businesses deal with production of a product, some relate to only the service industry and some deal only in selling and buying of finished goods. In the current economic activity changes, manufacturing and goods industries are somehow linked to services. This study is focusing on how service innovation and different models of service are helping and providing benefits to different business organizations as they attempt to enhance their profit, to retain their customers, to expand their business and to get a competitive advantage in the competitive business world in different countries. Different research methods have been invented, and many research projects are being taken into consideration. A huge amount of finances are being used on research and development departments in order to benefit from timely information that will help companies earn greater profits.

The study of Thakur and Hale (2013) gives a detailed view on service innovation and its positive effects on creating wealth and getting additional profit results. The study shows that the factors that are in control of organizations contribute greatly to the production of wealth in both Indian and US organizations that are following the same managerial policies. This study compared two different countries: the United States and India. Factors which are not under the control of the organizations or beyond the control of them are having a negative effect on financial conditions and on the profit ratio of businesses. There are two types of factors; some are internal factors, and some are external factors. Internal factors are those which are in control of the organization, and external factors are those which are not in control of the organization. Organizations are managing internal factors to get competitive advantages. An organization is competing by providing best services to its customers. Nowadays organizations not only deal with tangible products but also intangible products. Telecommunications, entertainment industry, the hotel industry and stock exchange are some of the examples of business organization which are dealing with services, although to a great degree the organizations which are dealing with tangible goods are linked to services.

Alam (2013) discussed the importance of customer interaction in India in innovating services. Alam argues that it is important to enhance service quality to sustain the customers and achieve a strong organizational financial position. This study examined the role of customer interactions in making strategies to enhance and innovate the service system of the organization in India and found that there is limited interaction with customers when making service innovation policies in many Asian countries including India. The sample size of this research was based on 24 service industries from which 48 managers were interviewed and 24 employees were interviewed to get a true picture of the result. The role of customer interaction has a vital importance in generating new policies, as they possess great importance.

All the efforts which are being made, all the policies which are being formulated and all the models which are being developed are just to facilitate the customers and capture more customers by expanding the business and by providing customers what they want in a more innovative and updated way. Nowadays different business organizations in India are competing on a quality and service basis each and every day. The organizations are getting advantages by providing their customers the best service and best finished product in the best suitable ways.

Service innovation in China

China is one of the countries leading the world in creating a number of inventions in its service industries and finding innovative ways to provide customers with quality products at the lowest price. China is bringing change in the process, in technology, in human resources policies and in the marketing strategy to enjoy surplus profit globally as well as domestically. Fan (2014) discussed that innovative capabilities, especially in China, are significantly related to the economic development. Although China is one of those countries that provides the best quality product at the lowest cost, it still needs to take certain steps regarding marketing policies to capture more customers Zhou and Li (2012). Zhou and Li argue that environment and demographic factors should be significantly considered in order to achieve success in the country where the services are provided.

To use the resources to an optimal level and to give its best to the customers, organizations in China are studying the factors of service innovations more closely. Examples of these factors are value chain system, customer interactions, channels of distributions products, and technological factor. These days, organizations are globally giving 100% to get a competitive edge by fulfilling the demand of customers before other organizations surpass them and meet the demand. For this purpose, Chinese organizations are investing in research and development and trying to make sure their departments are updated and informed about the current situation and demands of customers.

China is one of the developed countries which is dominating the world in different industries, whether it is smart phone or any other gadgets and software. There are also some different perceptions about the industries of China – that the products which are being provided are cheap in price and low in quality as well, but this perception represents a small portion of the industries of china. Huawei is one of the dominant companies which deals in selling network equipment and in making smart phones. It has also dominated some Western markets as well. Xiaomi is a company which caused a storm in the smart phone industry by providing updated quality design of its smart phone at a reasonable price.

Xiaomi used innovative service by selling the smart phone online which placed the company in the top 10 smart phone companies.

Alibaba is one of the largest top-selling online companies. It sells products online all over the world. Its gross income is much higher than any other online company. The level of success of this company indicates its innovative services. China is expanding to many Western countries by competing in cars, in software, in smart phone and in all kinds of gadgets. All this success is the result of service innovations policies, because in today's world the more you innovate the service, the more you get benefited and get more successful and get competitive advantage in the business world (Chen, Wang, Huang, & Shen, 2016).

According to the study of Williamson and Yin (2014), accelerated innovation is being followed by Chinese industrialists to compete in the business world. This study observed these innovations in different industries such as telecommunications, pharmaceutical companies and in e-commerce as well. Chinese industries and Chinese engineers are contributing their efforts to minimize the cost and to provide the best quality to customers by cutting the time of production. They are doing this by producing more in a given time, by following the approach of more efficient rather than effective production, and by giving the space for suggestions and feedback.

The location of the business has an important influence on the business environment. China is in the Asia Pacific region. Therefore, Chinese businesses get rapid access to growing markets in Pakistan and India. This good location helps China with the knowledge about customers' requirements and cost advantage. These are examples of how geographic presence influences business.

In addition to the preceding discussion about service innovation in China, the Olympic Games are a good example of the Chinese service innovation. In 2008 the Olympic Games in China was favorable for the country. Chinese businesses were able to compete with other game product manufacturers successfully. This brought high revenue into the country and contributed to the growth of the Chinese service sector and service innovation.

Service innovation in the United States

Service innovation study is a new concept; it gained maturity all of a sudden due to its importance and huge advantages. A lot of research has been conducted on lots of data. A lot of data has been analyzed by different scholars who contribute their knowledge by collecting data from different sectors such as the health sector, finance sector, manufacturing industry and service sector. This branch of knowledge was introduced in the 1980s and late 1990s, but with the passage of time it has emerged so fast that it became the center of attraction for all types of industries.

In the 1950s, the service sector of the US was assumed to have little or no productivity growth and was not capable of innovation. It was a sector with low-paying jobs, low levels of technological dependence and undeveloped business organizations. But in recent years the service sector of the US has been marked by tremendous growth. It is now an integral component of economic activity and growth. There is observable growth in Internet and Web-based services and high-technology environmental services, which indicates that in the United States the services are innovative and knowledge-intensive, therefore adding value to economic growth of the country (Thakur & Hale, 2013).

Various research studies have highlighted significant results related to service innovation in the United States. According to this research, service industries welcome innovation more than manufacturing industries. Service innovations are considered the best way to expand the business. Through service innovation, businesses can approach their customers all over the world through worldwide selling of products online or by managing their distribution channels properly and more effectively. The production process is involved with services directly and indirectly. Services include all the activities which help or support in production of goods, in distribution of goods and transporting of the finished products.

In the United States, research and development departments spend a lot of money to review models, to generate new models, and to build strategies that update customer needs. A lot of progress has been seen in US industries. The service business is observed as a more open innovator than manufacturing business. Manufacturing mostly follows formal models which are a barrier to change and innovation, whereas service industries are willing innovators that accept change, accept new ideas, accept new models and are ready to execute innovated policies (Ostrom, Parasuraman, Bowen, Patricio, & Voss, 2015).

In recent years, the United States has been observed as a country involved in the exchange of services rather than products. The service industry in the United States is observed to be shaping the traditional structure of organizations as well as having a great influence on people's lifestyle in indoor and outdoor activities. In the past, people bought goods by personally visiting different markets or retail stores and getting information from experienced and knowledgeable people. Today, in this time of innovation in service, people can get to know the product on the internet. It has been observed that people are browsing different sites which are related to the service and sector they're interested in. It could be the hotel industry, manufacturing industry or entertainment industry. All they need to look for is a relevant site where there is accurate information regarding price, discounts and promotion options. With a click of a button or a blink of an eye, service innovation has changed buying style, selling style, and it has saved people a lot of time.

Different social websites such as Facebook, Twitter, Google and YouTube are considered to be the best places to advertise products and get feedback from people so that sellers can develop the best policies to innovate their product. These social media websites are used by many industries to advertise verities of products to give the customers good space to select what they want. People can make cost analyses easily and place their order according to what they desire online. Thus, with the breakthrough of a different service, innovation has caused great impact on businesses as well as on people's lives.

Microsoft, Apple and Uber are the prime example of service breakthroughs in the last couple of decades. Uber is a service providing company that provides transportation services to people whenever and wherever they want. The owner of this company observed the gap in service to consumers, noted the business research, captured the opportunity and is now earning a huge amount of profit worldwide. This company is also planning to get into another service business, providing home delivery of food from restaurants.

After the economic recession period from 2007 to 2009 customers' spending gradually increased as people became more confident about their financial future. When people have the confidence that their income will be maintained or increase, they spend more on items like furniture and cars and their accompanying services. The increased spending has increased the need for services in the United State which in turn has increased the new developed enhanced services.

Service innovation in Germany

Germany has extended its High-Tech Strategy (HTS) to the new Comprehensive High-Tech Strategy 2020. This strategy adopted by Germany indicates that global challenges for that country are climatic changes and growth in population. These challenges call for action in order to make the economy secure and to enable it to develop further (Harrison et al., 2014). The aim of HTS is to secure economic, social and cultural growth and development. The HTS has the objective to achieve these goals by developing specific service sectors. Germany emphasizes improving the cooperation between science and the service industries and advanced support to create an innovation environment.

For service innovation, organizations should show collaborative efforts and include all of their employees and customers. Based on this strategy, employees and customers should be incorporated into the existing service innovation practices. Hence, service innovation in German companies is marked by integration of managers, employees and customers. The role of customers is a key factor in helping Germany to grow their service innovation process, especially in ideas evaluation, determining the source of innovation, and service innovation investment decision.

According to recent data, in 2016 it was estimated that the government and German industry and science has spent approximately 92 billion euros on research and development. This amount is equal to approximately 3% of Germany's GDP. As compared to other European countries, they spent approximately 2% of their total GDP on research and development. It is estimated that by 2025 Germany's annual spending on research and development will increase by 3.5% (Drucker, 2014). The study shows figures on how Germany's services are active and innovative. One of the indications is the number of registered patents; there were 371 registered patents in Germany in the year 2015. This number is relatively high when compared to the registered patents in the US in the same year, which was 200 and in China, which was 27. Another indicator is the total money spent in production and service innovation; Germany had spent 160 billion on that by 2016.

Political influences refer to the ideas that are generated from different political parties. There are a number of different political parties in Germany. Each group has ideas about how to best regulate businesses and how to protect consumers' and employees' welfare and rights. These parties are supporting innovation not only in the service sector but also in the production sector.

Science is valued in Germany, and sales of scientific publications have increased by one billion euros in the last 20 years. In 2016, 1,367 publications were published. This indicates that German firms and scholars are more interested in innovation including service innovation.

To bring it all together, the strong connection between politics, industry and science has helped the development of service innovation in Germany and has increased its progress.

Service innovation in Canada

From the list of OECD countries, Canada is characterized by a holistic system of R&D in services that is consistent with industry practices. R&D in the Canadian services is growing more rapidly as compared to R&D in other business sectors of Canada. The available facts and figures depict that efforts for innovation in the Canadian service sector and indicate a significant role of services in the economy. The major R&D portion of the Canadian budget is spent on service innovation. Approximately 30% of total R&D in the Canadian business sector represents the private sector service industries.

Canadians adjust themselves in an era which is marked with slow growth and rapid changes.

Innovation in Canada has been prioritized in three different categories:

- People: This part of innovation includes the way more people in Canada are capable to acquire the skills and experience related to global demands and according to the requirements of the digital economy.
- Technologies: This category of development in innovation includes the methods for Canada to adopt emerging technologies that create jobs and industries. Technology innovation also compels Canada to focus on the great wave of global innovation.
- Businesses: The major part of innovation in Canada focuses on service innovation in order to remain globally competitive.

Discussion and analysis

In service innovation, service management theory that supports customer involvement is very important. Service firms rarely engage customers in innovation activities due to the issue of imitation by the competitors in the industry.

But due to globalization, there is intense competition in the service industry. This competition has compelled the service firms to seek innovation for survival in both developed countries like the United States and in the emerging countries like India.

There was a little need for innovation before the time of economic liberalization in India, particularly in the service industry, as at that time India was an inward-looking economy lacking in intense competition around the globe. Later, after economic liberalization, enterprises in India started exploring innovation in their processes. The increased competition drove innovation. Deregulation increased the competition in both India and the United States, forcing the businesses to innovate. As a result, innovation became a key activity in the service industry of both economies.

Comparing Brazil's innovation in service in terms of macroeconomic variables shows that Brazil remains below the most innovative countries. In 2014, China entered into the ranking in the category of innovative countries. Both China and Brazil are BRICS countries, but both countries are traditionally low in ranking in service innovation as compared to developed countries. From 2001 to 2013, the intensity of R&D in China has been increased from 1% to 2%, which is considered to be significant growth. This shows that China has put a lot of resources into R&D in order to innovate in the service sector. Now the R&D intensity of China is higher than that of the European Union as a whole. The entrepreneurs in China now heavily rely on innovations for fulfilling local demands (Zhu & Euchner, 2018).

Management has to face a number of challenges related to innovation in the business. They have to decide what to change or innovate, how the innovation should be brought in the organization and how to make people aware about the concept of innovation within the organization. The Canadian, Brazilian, German, United States, Chinese and Indian business environments face several different challenges such as adverse culture not supporting innovation and lack of funds for innovation.

It is also very challenging for a business to develop the innovation in the business. For innovation to be a core competency and a tangible cultural value, there should be an appropriate degree of consistency between the organizational processes, metrics, reward structures and top management behavior.

The above-mentioned economies experienced sustainable growth for many years after the recent recession period. These countries are in the main strong economies in the world. Therefore, their businesses get rapid access to the global growing markets. Their social factors have also a significant influence on their service innovation. Different social trends tend to enhance or suppress the demand and supply of the services. The governments of these economies have different supportive laws and regulations related to service innovation and their political parties have a positive influence on the business environment.

Now there is a new trend of outsourcing innovation and IT facilities. Research has revealed that information systems or information technologies have now been widely outsourced by many organizations – the world's outsourcing totals approximately $150 billion (Gonzalez, Gasco, & Llopis, 2005). It was forecasted that this market value is increasing, and firms are increasing their expenses of outsourcing in order to facilitate IT-related services.

The information technology outsourcing (ITO) has an increasing impact on all major organizations, and this will gradually become an integral part of any organization's strategy and business activity. ITO is a global trend, and now globalization is marked with some distinct determinants which are evolving the technology and also have reformed the marketplace and given rise to a new era of digitization. For sustainable business advantage, businesses will have to adopt digitization and employ technology experts to explore it. The era of digitization includes web and broadband communication which enables the organization to fulfill the needs of the digital world. This shows that IT has now become an important part of business activities.

The present study would propose and discuss the major reasons and risks involved in outsourcing of information technology (IT). This study is devoted to identifying the reasons and risks associated with outsourcing of IT, what the main reasons are that make organizations outsource IT functions and what the risks associated with outsourcing are.

Why IT outsourcing

Different research studies have highlighted that there are a number of possible reasons for a businesses to outsource their IT activities. Businesses are gaining immediate long-term benefits by outsourcing IT support services. Some of the benefits or reasons for businesses to outsource their IT services are explained in the sections that follow.

Saving the staff cost

Development of a large in-house IT department is very expensive. It includes not only capital costs but also training and maintenance costs. Outsourcing allows people outside the business who are specialists in IT management to hire, train and retain highly professional IT staff to serve the business. In this way, the outsourced high IT specialists do not need to be permanent staff members of the business (Alner, 2001). To remain competitive in the market, it is important that the business should acquire and identify the knowledge of information systems. But the effort to retain permanent employees with a high level of knowledge is very difficult today. Also, updating training is very expensive for the business, so outsourcing is essential (Olson, 2007).

Reduction in IT cost

Installation of a complete IT infrastructure, which includes the networks, servers, wiring, security and other components, is very expensive. When the businesses outsource the IT support, they are able to convert their fixed cost into variable cost and provide a cushion for cost reduction. Usually the cost of maintaining and providing the service of IT exceeds the costs of the outlay, so at this time the outsourcing is advisable.

Service providers of IT services are exposed to different kinds of risks and problems, and a vast amount of knowledge and skills are required for resolving these problems. The main focus of service providers is the provision of IT services to the clients. Therefore, they dedicate all their resources and capacity to provide the IT services; in this way they are able to gain economies of scale (Smith, Mitra, & Narashimhan, 1998). Further, these economies of scale are transferred to the client in the form of lower prices for achieving the same services by outsourcing (Hayes, Hunton, & Reck, 2000).

Provision of uninterrupted flow of service

In the globalization era, the technology is evolving and becoming more complex, and management of hardware and software programs is very challenging. Within a developed industry of sales and marketing, it is required by the businesses to have innovative hardware and software programs to cope with the competitive industry. Businesses also require strong networking and a continuous flow of service of internet with the exclusive support of intranet and extranet. It is complex and expensive for the businesses to provide all these services; on the other hand, the professional IT network service providers have expertise in providing such complex technicalities.

Inhibit anxiety

When business disasters or related service failures are dealt with competently and with expertise, there is less anxiety among the employees of the organization. These challenges include the failure of an internet or crash of a computer and so on. These are not only physical disasters but also highly emotional issues for the employees, as they are related to their work efficiency. Employees are worried about the loss of their productivity, and they are threatened by the data security and fear of deletion of information. When the IT professionals are skilled workers of the service providers, they handle these problems smoothly and don't create panic in the business environment.

By implementing successful service innovation, companies in the strong economy countries develop significant competencies of providing service coverage, developing proper promotions for the customers, and easing the process of service delivery. Coverage of service is referred to as offering various services to existing clients and maintaining a good relationship with them. Development of services is referred to as focusing on a company's ability to grasp the service opportunities. Service process management is a company's ability to deliver service while continuing to innovate with new service offerings.

Believing in innovation is significant for the organization, but it is not equal to being innovative. Often organizations are not willing to invest in developing an innovation capability that remains in the organization for decades and transforms the organization. Different organizations have features which can be utilized for institutionalizing innovation, changing the mind-sets and combining with appropriate tools for creating innovation as a success in the organization.

There is no standard procedure for achieving innovation within the organization. Each organization has different goals and objectives related to innovation. There are different processes, systems and constraints in each organization. Hence, service organizations should develop the right capabilities that match their organization's values and culture to help service innovation.

For developing innovation, it is critical that the organization to have innovative infrastructure, the talent, and a management which supports creative ideas for making success stories within the organization. Most companies claim that they encourage creativity, risk taking and rule breaking in the organization, but it is management infrastructure and corporate culture that actually put constraints on these activities. Innovation is not only a systemic capability in the organization, nor it is a core value that is deeply instilled in the corporate culture. It is also a capacity of an innovator in the organization who fight heroically in the organization to push his creative ideas forward (Mina, Bascavusoglu-Moreau, & Hughes, 2014).

For service innovation to be a core competency and a tangible cultural value, there should be an appropriate degree of consistency between the organizational processes, metrics, reward structures and top management behavior. The top management support is significant for innovation in the organizational process. If the top management is not supportive, then it is difficult to get the resources required and to involve the stakeholders in the activities with an aim of developing innovation capabilities.

In many organizations, service innovation is still compelled to remain alive as a disconnected silo only loosely associated with new product development, an incubator or a new venture division. In these circumstances, innovation is not involved in the rest of the processes and operations of the organization, and the innovation silos produce limited ideas that never make a meaningful impact on the profits of the company.

For the organizational structure which is important for innovation, it is needed that organization should adopt the social systems or institutional structures that have proven to be most favorable for innovations that occur in places like Silicon Valley in the United States.

It is also very challenging for a business to develop the innovation in the business. For innovation to be a core competency and a tangible cultural value, there should be an appropriate degree of consistency between the organizational processes, metrics, reward structures and top management behavior.

To improve and increase service innovation, universities should provide practical exposure to their students to learn innovation and its implementation in private and public sectors. By doing so, universities will reduce the shortage of entrepreneurship skills and enhance the collaboration with public sector, government and business organizations. In addition, universities as well as business organizations will get more funding from the government for the purpose of doing research on service innovation.

Developing a steady pattern of innovation thinking behavior is important to develop the culture of service innovation. This can be done through educating the managers and the practitioner in service organizations to focus on integrating innovation thinking into their management methods and philosophies.

References

Alam, I. (2013). Customer interaction in service innovation: Evidence from India. *International Journal of Emerging Markets, 8*(1), 41–64.

Alner, M. (2001). The effects of outsourcing on information security. *Information Systems Security, 10*(2), 1–9. https://doi.org/10.1201/1086/43314.10.2.20010 506/31401.6

Carlborg, P., Kindström, D., & Kowalkowski, C. (2014). The evolution of service innovation research: A critical review and synthesis. *The Service Industries Journal, 34*(5), 373–398.

Chen, K. H., Wang, C. H., Huang, S. Z., & Shen, G. C. (2016). Service innovation and new product performance: The influence of market-linking capabilities and market turbulence. *International Journal of Production Economics, 172*, 54–64.

Drucker, P. (2014). *Innovation and entrepreneurship*. Routledge.

Fan, P. (2014). Innovation in China. *Journal of Economic Surveys, 28*(4), 725–745.

Gonzalez, R., Gasco, J., & Llopis, J. (2005). Information systems outsourcing risks: A study of large firms. *Industrial Management & Data Systems, 105*(1), 45–62.

Gil-Garcia, J. R., Helbig, N., & Ojo, A. (2014). Being smart: Emerging technologies and innovation in the public sector. *Government Information Quarterly, 31*, I1–I8.

Harrison, R., Jaumandreu, J., Mairesse, J., & Peters, B. (2014). Does innovation stimulate employment? A firm-level analysis using comparable micro-data from four European countries. *International Journal of Industrial Organization, 35*, 29–43.

Hayes, D. C., Hunton, J. E., & Reck, J. L. (2000). Information systems outsourcing announcements: Investigating the impact on the market value of contract-granting firms. *Journal of Information Systems, 14*(2), 109–125.

Lopes, D. P. T., & Barbosa, A. C. Q. (2014). Management and organizational innovation in Brazil: Evidence from technology innovation surveys. *Production, 24*(4), 872–886.

Lusch, R. F., & Nambisan, S. (2015). Service innovation: A service-dominant logic perspective. *MIS quarterly, 39*(1).

Mina, A., Bascavusoglu-Moreau, E., & Hughes, A. (2014). Open service innovation and the firm's search for external knowledge. *Research Policy, 43*(5), 853–866.

Moser, M., de Oliveira, M. A., & Bueno, R. L. P. (2017). Comparison between Brazil and the 30 most innovative countries in the world. *EMAJ: Emerging Markets Journal, 7*(2), 19–28.

Olson, D. L. (2007). Evaluation of ERP outsourcing. *Computers & Operations Research, 34*(12), 3715–3724.

Ostrom, A. L., Parasuraman, A., Bowen, D. E., Patricio, L., & Voss, C. A. (2015). Service research priorities in a rapidly changing context. *Journal of Service Research, 18*(2), 127–159.

Rodionova, I., & Epifantseva, A. (2017). Positions of the BRICS countries in world economics innovation. *Studia Ekonomiczne, 323*, 107–117.

Smith, M. A., Mitra, S., & Narasimhan, S. (1998). Information systems outsourcing: A study of pre-event firm characteristics. *Journal of Management Information Systems, 15*(2), 61–93.

Thakur, R., & Hale, D. (2013). Service innovation: A comparative study of US and Indian service firms. *Journal of Business Research, 66*(8), 1108–1123.

Williamson, P. J., & Yin, E. (2014). Accelerated innovation: The new challenge from China. *MIT Sloan Management Review, 55*(4), 27.

Zhou, K. Z., & Li, C. B. (2012). How knowledge affects radical innovation: Knowledge base, market knowledge acquisition, and internal knowledge sharing. *Strategic Management Journal, 33*(9), 1090–1102.

Zhu, H., & Euchner, J. (2018). The evolution of China's innovation capability: An interview with Hengyuan Zhu Hengyuan Zhu talks with Jim Euchner about the many ways innovation practices are being adopted, adapted, and reinvented in China. *Research-Technology Management, 61*(3), 11–15.

5   The future of service innovation

Service innovation performance: current status and trends

Service innovation of late has become a matter of grave concern, and it involves not a single industry but has taken over a larger group. Therefore, service innovation has begun to occur more often in various contextual forms. The forms include both radical, a new range of services, or incremental, which are bringing enhanced improvements to existing range of services.

Although the process of service innovation is restricted entirely to the service sector, however, this is not necessarily the correct connotation of the term. There are several types of new and improvised set of services which have the non-service sectors included in them. These sectors comprise manufacturing firms that work towards enhancing the supply systems through the addition of valued services. In the same manner, the entire process of service innovation has little or no relationship with products, especially there is no intangible nature inside the product innovations.

It is a significant point to note that services are customized in accordance with the needs of individual customers and may also consist of several stakeholders. Speaking of the knowledge-intensive sector, service innovation and development has a major role to play, which cannot be undermined. Service innovation here has altogether a different connotation and intelligibly different from product innovation.

The focus on technological advancements and the concentration of the innovation activities around the research and development departments does not clearly define the concept of service innovation. In several instances, various ideologies are put into place for defining service innovation, but there is no concrete definition that puts together everything in one place.

The "four-dimensional model", however, describes the idea of service innovation, albeit relative to the knowledge-based industry. This model considers the dimensions as follows:

- Concept of new service in the market;
- The new delivery system, which gives judgment on how the services are rendered to the end users;

- Use of enhanced technology, ensuring efficient delivery of systems to the end users;
- Interface of client that refers to innovative ways where clients involve themselves in service production.

Apart from multidimensional characterizations, which involve service innovation, there are various methodologies in which service innovation takes place and goes up to levels of development. Most prevalent processes involved in service innovation include:

- Internal service innovation processes which have the unintentional and incremental innovations with respect to the existing nature of services;
- Internal service innovation projects which focus on ameliorating service production systems and the relevant content thereof;
- Service innovation projects focused on testing the new ideas with the customers;
- Innovation projects that are custom-designed to meet the individual needs of customers in a particular set of environments;
- Service innovation in the projects that have been funded through some external means, and this includes the research-oriented collaborations, where focus is always on generating new concepts and developmental platforms.

Innovation in the service model is an intangible product and an innovative means with clear-cut development. The innovation continues to develop and upgrade itself over a period of time. For instance, a manufacturing company has the thought of selling a service agreement with a service company. The service company will involve itself in the development of new service-based products into the market through this agreement. When looking to this example in the context of a service model, both companies seem to be innovative, although to varied extents. Service innovation in this example presents a growing innovation in the service industries, irrespective of the novelties and the degree of novelties. If the agreement is big the manufacturing company in this example was servitized. Hence, more service industry organizations are responsible for a major increase in employment across the other wider industry groups. This example discusses the importance of servitization involved within the manufacturing industries.

Despite being broadly documented as an engine of growth and highly competitive in nature, service industries are less talked about and far behind in comparison to the extent of knowledge and impact made on introducing concepts of innovation within the manufacturing sector.

The influence of service innovation is linked to the technological approach to innovation. However, the technological approach to innovation is wide and significantly influenced by the rapid changes in technology which lead to create service innovation gap in services while trying to cope with the speed of technological change.

One of the current statuses of service innovation is that services have not yet been paid the proper attention from policy makers and business organizations. One of the many reasons why services have not been given their proper share of credit and innovation is because of the lower levels of service research and development, lower intensity, and fragile patenting system.

The service economy perhaps innovates more than the value indicators are likely to suggest, and somewhere there is hidden or invisible innovation in service economies which stand to be clearly identified and subsequently supported by nothing else but fitting public policies. Therefore, the service-dominated countries have started focusing on the relationships, intangible resources, and production processes for co-creating the value through servitization.

The service innovation model cannot work on the concept –"one-size-fits-all" for the simple reason that the service sector considers a variety of sub-industries that have differences related to the extent of knowledge-intensiveness needed for innovation. In this context, it becomes necessary to know the fundamental discrepancies that are known to exist inside the innovation patterns across the service sector firms.

There are few scholars engaged in research and development activities in different innovative firms, especially in the financial sector. The amount of money involved in service innovation and its R&D expenditures, such as procurement of machinery and software and equipment, is relatively low compared to the amount of money invested in innovation in the manufacturing industry. Services, which seem to fall in the category of extremely high innovation, require a lot of expenditures. In such types of innovation, there is a need to conduct huge research and development activities using verities of skilled people and wide range of competences.

Organizations in service industries show higher levels of cooperation in the process of innovation among each other, in contrast to the manufacturing industry. For example, this is quite true in the case of the business financial sector, though there are also many similar behaviors shown in several other types of service subsectors.

Open collaboration in the service industry leads to the development of different open innovations. Open Services innovation pushes manufacturing organizations to make the transformation from the current product-oriented models of businesses towards the service-oriented business. By doing so, manufacturing industries will sustain or increase their competitive advantages.

There are not one but many different types of case studies in the support of the evidence and data for the joint products and services factors, and all of these embrace new business models. As far as measurement of service innovation is concerned, there is the need for the process approach. In this type of measurement, the innovation is seen as an ultimate outcome, considered insufficient because there is no involvement of intangible character involved inside the service innovation through which means the actual type of service is delivered in collaborating with the end user, or the client.

The change from a solo act of selling products, which are tangible to the end customers, involves a comprehensive process of customer involvement, and this has largely influenced the ways of innovation in different ways.

Importance of typology in service innovation

Reviewing the process of innovation requires systematic review on large scale, which is done through either of these means:

- Extraction of data
- Systematic synthesis
- Assessment of the quality
- Comprehensive products and services research

There are many studies that clearly point out the innovation findings in both manufacturing and service sectors. The findings have determined that services have an increased innovation rate compared to the manufacturing sector. The findings have also related the increase of service innovation to the availability of the innovation instruments and the cost of innovation development. Instruments of service innovation are becoming more readily available all the time. For example, the biggest services innovators, such as Amazon and Alibaba, needed only an internet connection to develop their innovative market. To implement service innovation is less costly in most of cases than implementing manufacturing innovation. That is because implementing manufacturing innovation needs more machinery and effort than service innovation.

It is worth pointing out that service innovation adds cumulative values to the services more than with manufacturing innovation. This can be measured through how service innovations are unique and their relevance as we talk of the innovations in cash machines, online banking, e-commerce and even pizza delivery. Self-service shops and cafes show how important they are with respect to services.

To explain further, in the case of the IT services, strategic and perfectly designed applications have been developed to facilitate information exchanges between service providers and their clients. These applications are interfaces that are becoming the key focus of service innovation.

Many studies have also tried to apply the process of typology to service innovation. The typology was extensively used in the scholarly work on manufacturing innovation and on innovation as a general phenomenon. However, when it comes to service innovation it is not always simple to classify them into product or process category. The intangibility characteristic of services does not help to develop this kind of classification. Therefore, studies should focus on alternative typologies to address service innovation classification away from the dominant typologies that were built on manufacturing and goods characteristics. The relatively new emerged alternative typologies such as open innovation, disruptive innovation and market innovation can address service innovation more comprehensively and practically than previous typologies.

Organizational innovation is also interrelated with service innovation, though in the process of organizational innovation, there are several types of innovative changes taking place within the organizational structure. These innovative changes are not only restricted to changes brought about in procedures.

Innovation in service sector indicates systems and agents

What are the systems?

The study of services innovation has been progressively and genuinely relative to the presence of innovation systems and closely connected networks. Service innovation now is being seen as a major factor in the development of business. Innovations in the service industry sector are the result of staging of competitive environments, where stand-alone performing agents begin to examine strategies defined by others, and where using a range of informational and variety of other sources is used in organizing their innovative efforts.

In addition to the above argument, there is also the perception that there are many other types of innovations which are due to a variety of collaborative activities that are far beyond the skills of hard work and astute thinking of entrepreneurs, ground-breaking firms and inventors.

Now these collaborative activities can take the shape of joint ventures or outcomes of the joint research and development projects. In this context the following generalizations are made:

- There are a few producer services, which play a decisive role, working as the intermediaries within the network of innovation systems, and this holds true in the case of technology-based services.
- There are also a few services which are closely connected and aligned within the innovation systems. These types of services play more significant roles as harbingers of innovation over small and large supply chains.
- Many services are linked within the framework of technology-oriented innovation systems. In this case, the key systemic impetus to innovation received by such types of services is potentially weak, coming directly from the professional associations and almost the same types of network structures existing out there.

The historical propensity of various services trying to make their way through supplier-driven innovative dawdlers may have resulted in an inheritance that some firms working within the ambit of these sectors are struggling to overcome. From this, the references can be easily drawn that in terms of the innovation systems, the institutional and informal structures supporting innovation are relatively slow compared to the manufacturing sector. However, it is also evident that the systems involved in production of knowledge resources have less orientation towards services innovation.

Besides, the Knowledge-Intensive Business Services (KIBS) do not enjoy the legacy of having well-linked connectivity within the structures of innovation networks. In this league, a new technology-based KIBS shows remarkable difference and good levels of variation from more traditional firms. Larger service firms, certainly, appear well networked in comparison to the smaller ones.

Large service firms in several sectors are showing an important role as the principal means to orchestrate innovation and differentiation in supply chain management. And this drives innovations in the field of manufacturing, like the railway companies, which have control and manipulate activities of suppliers of locomotives and railway carriages. Innovation in the large IT systems, such as the ones used in the banks to control ATMs and networks, should have the same level of connection to the general innovation systems as manufacturing firms.

Service innovation in high-technology sector

Service innovation is a continuously evolving concept, which in recent times is being studied within the ambit of service management research. This trend is part of various issues within the service industry. The recent issues arising out from customer involvement, cooperation, services specific measurement and transformation in knowledge.

Within the service industry sector, there is overgrown and extensive research examining the high service technology industry, service knowledge acquisition and small-and-medium service enterprises (SMEs) as well as integration of customer interaction in service operations.

The essence and concept of service innovation, which entered the spotlight in 1989, considers innovation as process of creating value through adding services to product offering. This process was developed to meet high demand. Innovation in services is also designed as the new process of service product that grow as a new procedure for service delivery.

Service innovation has specific importance in the high-technology sector, especially as it becomes a prominent source of competitive advantage gain. The importance increases because of the extensive competition and the challenged customers' demands and satisfaction. These factors push manufacturers and service providers to try to innovate distinctive services. This is typically the reason of the intensive high-technology sector innovation. In addition, it is the same reason that is pushing the high-technology sector organizations to develop a strong innovation system and integrate it into their process.

How does the service innovation take place and how it will be changed in the future?

The process of service innovation comes out of the uncertain environment of the manufacturing industry. The concept of service innovation in the past was built on the manufacturing goods industry logic. However, the distinctive characteristics of service, such as intangibility characteristics, have developed a different type of innovation related only to service operations and management. This different approach looks into various types of services, service business development, service operations, service marketing and service customers. In the future this trends will continue to develop a complete comprehensive innovation system applies to majority of services away from goods innovation systems.

Five important characteristics of service innovation defined

Characteristic 1

Service innovation is a shared process. There are newly developed concepts and many types of related business processes which have been developed within shared as well as interactive processes with the service provider as well as customers. Service innovation out here works as the means of co-production and co-innovation. There are also various types of service innovations which work according to the change in the division of labor. An example of that could be the introduction of self-service concepts such as electronic banking, online check-in and integration of various additional services within a range of products.

Characteristic 2

Although a lot of service innovations are still linked to the goods, it is still harder to judge those innovations before the customers get involved with their feedback.

Characteristic 3

Innovations in the service sector that have an architectural nature. Concepts of service innovation as evident in the case of group maintenance, or self-servicing in health care or telecommunicating services are the result of combinatory nature. Here again, the nature of combinatory roles needs careful analysis on different levels.

Characteristic 4

An increase in the requirements of the replication and scaling procedures. In comparison to the goods-based innovations, the service-based innovations do not have a defined replication or reproduction system. This characteristic is because of the high customers' involvement in service process and the different customers' perceptions.

Characteristic 5

Service innovations in the case of the distributed innovation effort occur due to the result of nothing else but the process of goods distribution systems. Here the service innovations are not due to the occurrence within the traditionally dedicated environments but due to the needs of distributions of goods.

The future of service innovation ✐

The world is changing fast, and this change is making the need for innovation more important than ever. The service industry is one of the key spheres where innovation cannot be ignored on any level. Innovation is always necessary to address the situation, which is important in conducting business and satisfying customers.

The future of innovation in the service sector holds relevancy from the fact that it will create seemingly new and improved methods for design and production of services, which will benefit customers. Most obviously, the future of service innovation will be based on expertise (both personal as well as technological), using a specific set of techniques at specific periods of time within service organizations.

In this context, the future of service innovation holds a multiplicity of dimensions and new strategies that create new opportunities for the organizations involved in the service delivery. When we talk of service innovation, it is a new or renewed kind of service offering a wide range of benefits to the customers and service providers in a broader context.

Service innovation is not only restricted in literal sense to the technical or mechanical processes that pave the way toward the creation of new ways of fulfilling the demands and needs of society. With innovation in the service sector, industries now and in the future will involve themselves in creating new demands and controlling the current customers towards the new demands.

Service innovation is again not only having a limited use relative to service innovation processes but also involves various types of subtle response systems, unwritten laws and practices, which become essential in accommodating, facilitating and accelerating the entire system. Therefore, service firms will be involved in a different type of competition – the competition of controlling customers' behaviors to creating new demands.

A significant part of innovation in services includes the "soft" or non-technological aspect, even when all of it appears to be in a restrictive interface of the products and processes. However, there is always innovation going on in the soft products. In a few service categories, specifically the information, technology holds the significance in shaping services. As far as process innovation is concerned, it is more technologically oriented.

Today, both the information and the communication technology industry are dependent on the fact that more and more of these industries are increasingly associated with other companies to add to the competitive global business environment.

Companies engaged in the service sector either directly or indirectly are adopting ground-breaking and open ways for developing innovative services or mixing their ongoing technologies for the purpose of supporting their service requirements and bringing much-needed refinement.

In this way, demand is created for the processes, methodologies and guidelines, which will further gauge and develop new service solutions. After the quickly changing business dynamics, more and more of the companies are engaging themselves in the processes wherein they have defined specific models and seek leverage from various kinds of collaboration networks using supply chain networks, business ecosystems or regional clusters with the sole purpose of complementing their services. One of the key advantages of the formation of collaboration networks is the enhanced accessibility offered to existing resources, which are otherwise not owned by the organizations.

Research done on service innovation with respect to the diversified set of actors as well as the technology-based value co-creation process turns out to be multidisciplinary in nature.

Business networks and innovation in designing the service models are essentially based on the studies conducted in different areas involving business studies and the information systems in general. It is also evident here that service innovation focused on three specific research areas: Open Innovation, Service Design Research and Business Ecosystem.

Such core research fields have been conceptualized in different ways, and there are also wider viewpoints and different sets of conceptualizations. Business ecosystems and service models discussed in terms of organizational competition and convergence is useful in changing the capture value. In the current scenario, there is an ever- growing need for increasing the understanding of service and how to integrating them in the business ecosystems.

Open innovation considers to which the companies are exceedingly working in a cross-disciplinary set ups. When there is service innovation, the companies are ready to innovate on the processes and likewise interact with specific partners with the sole purpose of increasing the innovation process. With this type of approach, there is a concrete reason for the development in areas of product and service innovation.

The concept of service innovations within the business networks are further determined on the basis of cognitive closeness and the social structuring in the society. Value is only created when companies have in place concrete service design research. Above all, in the current socio-political conditions, a networked interaction with customers besides other stakeholders becomes a necessity, as this is going to define the pathways for improving the services.

A service design focus reiterates the ever-growing importance of value creation process in link to the customers' needs. Managing the process for service creation on the level of an ecosystem is what needs to be worked out, and this is where many of the service-oriented companies are working.

It is quite necessary to understand that in changing business ecosystems and multidisciplinary roles, service innovation has to have a clear definition links them to the ecosystems. Innovation is useful in creation of a valuable ecosystem. But the fact is that there are several challenges in the value creation of the business ecosystem, more often related to the organization of value chain, coordination of the choices and participation incentives.

The concrete actions are useful in creating value within the ecosystem that is later integrated into the business ecosystem, and this can further be added from another concept coming straight from the research done in service design and open innovation.

In addition, the evolution of the business ecosystem viewpoint could provide innovative directions for exploring the design of nothing new except the technology-based services from understanding the dynamics.

Service design underwrites the structure of co-creation of service value in small, medium and large businesses. In this context, the knowledge produced help in combining the service process with the ecosystems process.

Services and the service sector are progressively vital growth factors in the economy. However, it is quite important to understand that services do not seem to become a cure-all solution. The standardized services model itself cannot address competitiveness issues related to the manufacturing industry. That is because of the different nature of problems within the service sector. Therefore, a careful analysis had to be done on whether innovation models can be still applied to both manufacturing and service sectors or if the service innovation model has gained its complete independence. The long-standing traditional boundaries known to exist between manufacturing and services have started to be clear. The success of any organization or even a manufacturing process is directly dependent on service innovation such as design, marketing and logistics, and above all on the product-related after-sales services.

Different types of service firms are involved in manufacturing of items useful to the end users in many ways, but these firms are making serious efforts towards development of service offering through various means of distribution channels.

Service innovation is a significant tool and a change agent which has brought about significant changes in the economy, making the whole of the economy productive, creative and sensibly reactive to the needs of customers. With the innovation in the service framework, there is substantial growth potential in creating new innovation tools, which are effective in development.

Innovation in the service sector is an important growth factor in leading the markets to macroeconomic changes in a short time frame. There are structural and economic changes in the societies in terms of transforming the lifestyles based on the new services offers.

Technology in service innovation

There cannot be any denial of the fact that digital transformations will have wider impact on the manner in which services will be delivered to customers in the near future. The following sections present the ways in which service innovation is happening and likely to proceed in the future.

Comprehensive search criteria

When customers need information on services, the first option is s searching them online. This is where vendors should take the first step in providing a good level of information in a manner that it is easy to find. The technological tools are well prepared to help both customer and supplier to do an easy search.

Online chatting option

The development of chatbots is the latest in the service industry. End users find it efficient to chat to a robot program and to a human service representative. These chatbots are using a secured and extensive program made from the instructions to recognize the questions and also respond quickly with the answers. The chatbots are capable of managing unlimited conversations, and more importantly, answer the things in a fast and objective way. In service innovation, the chatbots provide quick solutions in dealing with most difficult customer issues.

Cloud computing

Service innovation has received a huge boost after the arrival of the cloud computing concept. Today, there are several cloud-based applications designed for IT service desk delivery, and each of these items works in the case of customer relationship management, remote network management, Help Desk and many similar modes. Innovation in the service model that works in a cloud environment offers a ready-made and convenient solution to store historical data, share the documentation and exchange log-files.

Augmented reality

This high-end innovation is still limited in the service industry, though in the near future, the use of augmented reality (AR) software will open up unlimited possibilities of using cameras on smart phones or tablets for detailed analyses and a lot of other things. With the help of AR software, one could recognize the image and connect the information displayed.

Virtual reality

Virtual reality (VR) is also a highly developed and innovative technology which is actively involved in the process of service innovation. In serving the interests of users, VR technology will be helpful in virtualizing an entire data center, which is going to make the operations far easier and more convenient.

Smart phone technology

The appearance of new and high-tech mobile phones have given more thrust to service innovation than ever. End users will use the advanced and efficient systems provided in their smart phones to improve the technology. This new generation technology has become more prevalent in the field of IT service, where interaction takes place between the IT engineers and end users. Smart phone apps are also helping companies to understand the psychology of users, which would further help in customizing the user experience on all levels.

Internet of things

The internet of things (IoT) has made it possible to monitor remotely in a real-time setup. In the traditional system of things, the engineer went out to the location to record a measurement, and later on the measurement was transmitted to the control center. It is now possible with the help of IoT to control the information and in real time. For example, with the innovative and smart metering system, end users do not need to record and report the usage of electricity. All of it is done remotely and gives consumers access via an online dashboard.

Need of digitization in service innovation

The rapid growth of technology and its quick change have made digitization one of the important factors characterizing service innovation currently and will continue to be in the future. An increasing number of innovations in digital marketing trends has undeniably produced a useful user experience which is even far more enriching.

Digitization: its essence in growth of service industry

There is no doubt that digitization brought huge changes not only in the growth and development of the service industry but practically in all types of industries. Integration of digital elements at every stage within the processes and within the framework of existing products and services has aimed at creating better and more creative user experiences on a larger scale. There has always been social values as well as economic value in holding on to the digital revolution and service innovation is one of the sectors affected positively by these values.

Innovative products and services have largely shown the importance of digital components on various levels in improving the services of the variety of sectors. This is clearly visible when a product is controlled remotely through the means of smart devices such as smart phones and tablets.

Digital components expand to other service sectors like health care, banking and financial services, travel and hospitality, too. Digitally empowered solutions have gone to the next step in creating amazing value in the service sector, and this value is multiplying at an enormous rate.

Service innovation through the internet has also brought about revolutionary changes in the manner in which services are being carried out and delivered on the microscopic and macroscopic levels. Digital platforms, no matter how they behave or exist, have been important drivers in minimizing and also eliminating the frictions which were evident earlier within the delivery and payment procedures. Today, due to the quality of services offered, companies have become responsive to the needs of end users.

Big data is being regularly mined, and plenty of options are available for customers and service providers to be used for their service practices and needs. Hence, Service innovation and the technological improvement brought through digitization has improved services business innovation.

Digitization in many places has become an innovative facilitator, guiding the teams through the process of innovation. There are several process tools, and apps are making it possible to innovate and share screen presentations on a larger framework and in a short span of time.

A whole brave new world is under way as a result of digitization, and this has led to digital communication with end users. The service innovation is therefore evident in a short span of time. The smart digital systems available today are predicting and controlling the end user experience and redefining the service industry on a larger front. The service industry and the innovation therein would further be amplified with the use of artificial intelligence and studying the market insights, customer needs and customer behaviors.

And finally, one question that from the context of the relevance of technological changes and their impact on service innovation – "Is service innovation completely separated from technology innovation or integrated with them?" This question related to service innovation has continued to persist in the minds of management, especially while discussing the rationale of the policy framework for service innovation.

It is very important to differentiate between the microeconomic and macroeconomic viewpoints about technology changes and service innovation. In the case of the macroeconomic viewpoint, establishing a relationship between technology market failure and service innovation failure is an emerging trend. In other words, countries, enterprises and international customers have started to rely on service as a technology activity.

Therefore, there are several macroeconomic efforts trying to understand and analyze the service innovation policies linked to technologies and online markets. In a general sense, technology of innovation, whether in the service or any other sector, has been one of the key changes that has led to the success stories of economic growth. In that, developed countries, in terms of technology, or the technology high-performing nations have successful service innovation.

Moreover, high levels of service innovation are also complemented by technologies in the manufacturing industry. Therefore, technology in the manufacturing sector is not created for service operations but plays a remarkable role in service innovation through the services that are linked to good products.

In addition to other interrelated factors, service innovation in the case of the manufacturing industry extensively uses the Knowledge-Intensive Business Services (KIBS). The industry employs the services of business consultancy groups to get through the process offering value-added services to their goods.

However, there are a few countries which are in the forefront of developing creative innovation strategies in the service sector and adapting to the new frameworks and policies related to technology. But this does not mean that changes are not taking place. Specific service-oriented innovation policies are under way for introducing the framework conditions which are encouraging the process of service innovation and development in manufacturing and service-oriented firms.

Women and future of innovation in service

Innovation has gradually become a way to lead economic development as well as a key towards a prosperous future. In order to enhance the innovative capacity of an economy, it is rational to take advantage of the whole society, that is, both men and women. Like all other features of work atmosphere, "innovation" is considered a gendered term which creates a hurdle for women while participating in innovative processes, particularly in "masculine" and male-dominated industry. Therefore, failure to involve women in the process of research, science and innovation development can be perceived as intolerable waste of human resources.

This gender-based dimension is intensely entrenched in the way we research and create innovations, affecting the overall process from production to market. However, the focus of research efforts in this field was not concentrated on a specific group in terms of their involvement in the innovation process, such as men and women. To fill this gap, there is a need to examine the influence of gender dimension on service. Specifically, to examine gender equality issues and how they are linked to service innovation process and service organization operations. It is essential to understand what factors affect the innovation and creativity of both men and women.

Ernst and Young (2015) revealed six megatrends that define our future. These include rising entrepreneurship, digital future, urban world, global marketplace, health reimagined and a resourceful planet. Digitization is expected to transform society, business, economies, culture and individuals. Rapid advancement in connected devices, cloud computing, data analytics and social media are changing the way of doing business. Also, integrated technologies into sales operations and product development require companies to adapt their sales processes, pricing strategies and distribution models.

The increased use of data volume, data connectivity and computing speed along with rapid advancement in artificial intelligence and computerized systems implies that robotic devices can do several tasks more efficiently, carefully and quickly than humans (Hajkowicz et al., 2016). Robotization is influencing many areas of society, including transportation, health care, armed force, police and many others. Computers are now taking over routine intellectual work which is resulting "job polarization" (employment loss in middle-class job category that requires middle- level skills).

Therefore, demand for medium-skill work has been reduced, whereas demand for mainly low-skilled workers and highly skilled is continuously growing. Cognitive routine work has been taken over by information technology such as administrative work, bookkeeping, calculation performance, product assessment and monitoring processes. These are all areas with a strong representation of females and for that reason, women should be prepared to change.

Freeman (2015), in turn, noted that robots (any kind of machinery ranging from computers to artificial intelligence) offer a good substitute for humans and hence can easily replace workers, even those with high skills. On one estimate, about 36% of total Finnish employment is at risk of digitization in the next five years. There have been a lot of arguments about so-called megatrends which are strongly linked with changes in the structure of societal trends factor too. Moreover, the social power of women is also changing. Men will play a more balanced role. According to existing research literature, the changing social role of women means that the number of influential women will increase. Women will have a more prominent role in the leadership and management of entrepreneurial businesses and companies. On the other side, role of men is also changing. Men's practices and attitudes are changing, as is their position in society and the workplace due to the change in the status of women.

To a large extent, the economic growth of Western countries comes from service sectors. However, empirical research on innovation has generally focused on manufacturing sectors, lacking attention to innovativeness and innovation in the public and private sectors. Recently, there has been a progressively improved interest in innovative studies in these service sectors. However, service innovation is not generally included in the majority innovative surveys (Canadian Innovative Survey, European Community Innovation Survey, BROS, and SIBS). The significance of this focus towards the manufacturing sector particularly is that it considered men being more innovative as compared to women. Therefore, there is a need to explore more deeply into gender labeling of innovation from both practical and theoretical perspectives, as there remained a lack of research focusing on different scopes of gender labeling in relation to innovativeness. Moreover, there are rare studies which have focused on innovativeness in female-gendered labeled industries (Nählinder, Tillmar, & Wigren, 2015).

Gender issues and their role in promoting innovation and entrepreneurship have increased in recent years. Although the role of women in activities related to innovation and entrepreneurship is significantly increasing, there is still a significant gap in attaining parity with men. However, the current megatrend offers a wide range of innovative potentials for women's entrepreneurship. Normally, women entrepreneurs work in service sector industries, where technology/digitization may renovate the industry environment, although it has been perceived that gender is a compelling structure in innovation process system. Based on the extensive literature on innovation and gender, Agnete Alsos, Ljunggren, and Hytti (2013) have discussed the research path in respect of gender differences and similarities in innovation as well as gendering process of innovation. Gender has a significant effect on how innovations are implemented. According to Agnete Alsos et al. (2013), a key issue that lead to the lack of studies on gender perspectives in innovation is innovation visibility. The role of gendering the innovation process has continued to be invisible because of the fact that the majority of research studies related to innovation focus on products, organizations or processes and not on people. However, it is not that gender is not relevant to innovation studies. Men and women both are the smallest part in the system of innovation, and all other organizational systems are only outcomes of these parts. The gender invisibility does not imply that they are not involved in innovation. Systems, processes and organizations are comprised of actors, and identification of these actors is a way to examine the role of gender in the process of innovation as a source of secret potential.

According to Delmont (2016), there is an increased disparity of women in the field of information technology as compared to men, particularly in IT executive leadership role. Despite significant growth in information technology, women are not growing with it. The National Center for Women in IT (NCWIT) stated that information technology is growing rapidly; however, women are not keeping pace. The literature showed that in information technology, women account for less than 10% of total IT jobs, whereas men hold 90% of them. Researchers have also observed that women in IT leadership face major challenges and obstacles. Moreover, a low percentage of women in the field of IT is also discouraging the feminine workforce, and therefore underrepresentation of women in the IT field has negative consequences for women pursuing IT studies at universities. This results ultimately in a reduced number of women in the IT sector. One of the issues associated with underrepresentation of women in IT is the cultural environment that exists within IT organizations comprised of a male-dominated environment. Some women try to integrate into IT culture by espousing masculine traits and characteristics in order to be accepted, but they are not accepted authentically because mostly they are perceived as aggressive and too heavy-handed.

These negative attitudes are manifested in greater depth as women advance to higher positions in IT. Therefore, men in the field of IT at technical levels and those at leadership positions have difficulty in accepting women as credible and worthy of leadership and authority. These stereotypes and behavior present barriers to women in the field of IT.

Foss, Woll, and Moilanen (2013), in turn, explained the reasons for women's underrepresentation in the process of innovation. According to their research, women are as innovative as men when it comes to generating new ideas, but their ideas are seldom implemented within the organization. The study further indicated that women also suffer from the absence of collegial support for execution of their innovative ideas.

Moreover, they also found that usually women are not considered as innovators and for this reason, their innovative ideas are not even responded to in the first place; often their ideas are perceived as low-grade compared to men's ideas, and consequently they never reach the execution stage. One key reason behind this could be in-built gender bias i policies created for innovation. Many scholars have discovered that studies focusing on differences and similarities between men and women in outcomes of innovation may be intrinsically gender-biased because they tend to focus on specific industries and disciplines that are men dominated. Women tend to focus on specialization in business sectors where innovation research is not very common, like professional services, retail trade and personal services. Kvidal and Ljunggren (2014) stated that there is a socially constructed notion that women are not innovative in industry while men dominated business industries are innovative. This is all due to the social awareness of emerging technology which is more often connected to men than towards women.

Hajkowicz et al. (2016) identified that in the future, individuals will have to create their own jobs and they will need entrepreneurship attitude and skills. In addition, service sector jobs which need skills related to social interaction and emotional intelligence will rapidly become significant. The development of technological competencies is changing supply chains, reforming the workforce as well as redefining jobs. The current dominance of the peer-to-peer (P2P) marketplace and the growth of platform economics within a globalized labor market categorized by business activity is expected to change the models of traditional employment.

The two concepts – innovation and gender – are conceptualized and defined in several different perspectives.

Gender-related differences have been widely studied with reference to entrepreneurship. A number of research studies explained a well-known statement about male and female entrepreneurship – that female businesses normally underperform in number of employees, sales turnover, and so on. Women business owners are, compared to men, expected to own fewer businesses and be less willing to plan expansion. They tend to invest smaller startup capital to start smaller businesses compared to men. Moreover, the value of businesses run by a woman is significantly lower as compared to the businesses run by men. Men are more willing to grow their business quickly, while female entrepreneurship normally prefer to work as part-time service organizations. Moreover, women are highly risk averse and do not spend much time on networking compared to men.

Another recent study (Joensuu-Salo & Sorama, 2016) examined the attitude of women entrepreneurs toward future megatrends and the innovation process in their businesses. This study have found that women's attitudes toward expected future megatrends and offering opportunities for women entrepreneurs are positive. These positive attitudes are associated with feminine traits and competency of women entrepreneurs, new ways of doing businesses, possibilities of firm growth and work and family integration. Women see several possibilities for their own businesses. They also feel that some attributes generally associated with women, such as empathy, will be more significant in the future as a source of innovation as well as a source of competitive advantage. However, the authors also found some negative attitudes related to well-being, loss of jobs and demand for more skills.

There are certain psychological aspects that hamper the innovation process for women entrepreneurs. For instance, current mental models have an impact on what innovation type they can do. Another factor of concern is the gendered structure of technology. Older women entrepreneurs are of the opinion that technology is typically an area for men and new innovation in the digital age needs technological abilities and understanding. However, significant differences exist between the older and younger emerging women entrepreneurs. Younger emerging women entrepreneurs see no difference between women and men with respect to technological abilities. This attitude may be due to the fact that an ongoing transition in society has already transformed notions related to innovation and technology for younger women entrepreneurs who are interested in learning. Therefore, it is important here to understand how innovation and technology are presented at different school levels. For instance, Eriksson (2014) revealed in his study how gender perspectives can create innovation in upper secondary school. However, studies on age are important to determine the role of the generation of older women on innovation and how to get them involved in the technology of service business. For example, the older women may need easy platforms to reflect their ideas about their own businesses and anticipated innovations.

According to van Acker, Wynen, and Op de Beeck (2017), the innovation climate in an organization portrays the support and opportunities which employees receive through promoting, creating and executing ideas in the workplace. They examined the gender role and some other possible determinants in explaining differences within the apparent innovation climate in the context of public sector employees. Although the public sector is normally perceived as a more feminine working environment, the results of their study show that women are not encouraged very much in the process of innovation compared to men. However, some other determinants such as red tape and service duration were found to influence employees' experiences of the innovation climate.

There are a limited number of studies that have been conducted in interdisciplinary topics, which include economics literature, management, and business in the field of social sciences. In these limited interpapillary studies, findings and reports have discussed the problem of underrepresentation of women in business sector and science. The findings of these pragmatic comparative studies showed that, generally, a clear statistical pattern exists about women's lesser involvement in developing industrial and scientific knowledge. However, more than 35% of overall researchers in the government sector and higher education in most of the European countries are women. One of the indicators that there are fewer females in science and academia compared to males is that female researchers account for less than 25% in many countries (Huyer, 2015).

The relationship between innovation process and gender is complex. Nevertheless, literature on research conducted in this area shows that this area needs to be further investigated because of its potential as a source of economic development. Research studies have confirmed that the innovation process is not impartial to gender. Gender's role is still not well recognized in the innovation process. Okon-Horodynska, Zachorowska-Mazurkiewicz, Wisla, and Sierotowicz (2016) identified that the role of gender in the innovation process is an important factor to help to understand the involvement of men and women in the process of innovation development. They noted that there is a little dissimilarity in the way men and women perceive the innovation process which leads to the difference in their role of participation. Women normally like to value ability in making decisions in different phases of innovation development, whereas men pay more often attention to focusing on tasks.

Generally, women believe that the ability of decision-making is important in the innovation process and whereas men believe that it is the ability which plays a determining role to learn and make use of knowledge. Alsos, however, provided a much broader view to novel questions that must be addressed in the research area of gender and innovation. He stated that the issue of power is critical in both feminist theory and gender research. The dominance of masculinity in innovation, as well as complications in starting innovation processes to embrace wider understanding of innovation process, can be perceived as the outcome from gender hierarchy embedded in gender structures of innovation. Research studies focused on individual women involved in the process of innovation only are not enough to describe the contemporary practices of women innovation. Rather, there is a need to further investigate the structural factors related to their career perspectives and innovative roles.

As often said, we live in uncertain, complex, volatile, ambiguous and changing times. The world of the future will demand dimensions that recently comprise only options. Hajkowicz et al. (2016) stated that there will be a need for new ways of planning, thinking, communicating, directing and managing. In the future, there will be an increased interest in soft skills of entrepreneurs and potential employees, such as organizational, personal and interpersonal skills. These skills are crucial in the future in terms of life success and career. Self-development and innovative thinking as professionals are factors that may often be absent in young employees.

A study by Joensuu-Salo and Sorama (2016) has strong implications in this field, as it focuses on the feminist view that women are not a common group. Therefore, they don't have permanent gender characteristics; they change with the change in the world. Different generations of women respond differently towards new opportunities.

Business communities dominated by men have resisted feminine domination for decades. In response to this resistance, prevailing gender stereotypes in networks, processes and policies related to innovation are also being challenged. For example, in the business of technology women entrepreneurs were pushed to believe that new technologies and digitization were only for men.

Feminist-based studies have identified how innovation concepts were developed to reflect strong male domination. This has been evidenced through the typology of innovation. Women entrepreneurs normally face challenges in financing their innovations. Private financiers and public support consider women's innovation less significant.

Former studies have confirmed the strong link between masculinity, engineering and science, and innovation. Recently, the innovation process has been widened in policy and research both to cover more areas than patent and technology and therefore includes open innovation and service sector innovation. It is vital to building awareness in the policy and research domain. If this fact is accepted – that innovation is critical to gain competitive advantages – businesses and nations are in need of improving their resource utilization. Therefore, excluding women from involvement in the innovation process is a waste of time. They need to be encouraged to implement the systems or actions which will allow women in making their contributions. Therefore, there is a need for a political agenda in creating awareness and knowledge in this field.

Digital transformation and the future of innovation

Digital transformation is an actively discussed point in today, but the idea of digital products, services and medium were already recognized in 1990s and 2000s. Today, nearly all initiatives of digital transformation are being constructed on so-called third platform technologies, including cloud, mobile, analytics/Big Data and social technologies. The innovation accelerators such as robotics, 3D printing, IoT, next-generation security and many others rely on the third platform and increase its competencies. In increasingly growing digital marketplace, they are considered key drivers of companies' growth. Digital transformation involves using digital technologies to reshape a business process to become highly efficient. The idea is using technology not only to duplicate current service digitally but using technology to change that service towards something considerably better. Digital transformation can involve a number of technologies, but the most discussed topic these days are the Internet of Things, Big Data, cloud computing and artificial intelligence (Auriga, 2016).

Currently, there is no largely accepted definition for digital transformation, and usually the term digital transformation and digitization are interchangeably used (Schallmo, Williams, & Boardman, 2017). However, according to Mazzone (2014), "Digital Transformation is a careful and ongoing digital development of a company, idea process, business model, or approach, both tactically and strategically". Companies which are leaders in digital technology use are called "digital masters". They vary not only in their ability but also in clear vision. They view digital transformation as a transformation opportunity, not a technology challenge. Instead of relying on adjusting current practices, they explore the ways to use the new available technologies to transform the way of doing business.

Digital technology is rapidly becoming significant in accomplishing business objectives, and its influential effects have led to radical transformation of industries overall. As a result, extensive interest of managers in managing digital transformation is not too surprising. As information is becoming digitally transformed and mobile devices speed up in processing and persuasiveness power, an architecture and arena of innovation is unlocked – one in which digital and physical components are joint. Digital transformation is widely influencing different industries, particularly the telecommunications, health care, banking, automotive and manufacturing sectors. It enables improved designs, innovation practices and new business models, and shapes how companies create value on the internet. Companies now can leverage healthy customer relationships and improve cross-selling prospects through effective digital transformation. The digital transformation is not only about obtaining and positioning the right technologies for the business purpose but is also about having a significant method for handling managerial issues like business efficiency, human resources and business process redesign. The existing literature has demonstrated that digital technologies offer wide opportunities for product/service innovation, which is difficult to predict and control.

Therefore, firms require dynamic tools to assist them in handling the emerging digital innovation processes. Past studies in electronic commerce and information systems have reported the impact of several isolated technological factors such as data integration, technology use, digital technologies types and non- technological aspects such as human resource management, digital leadership, business process management and digital transformation of businesses. Digital transformation has been debated for many years, but there is still an unclear definition for the digital transformation model – that is, how the business models should be digitally transformed and which instruments and phases need to be considered (Schallmo et al., 2017).

Bharadwaj, El Sawy, Pavlou, and Venkatraman (2013), stated that, during recent years, business infrastructure is now digitized with improved interrelations between processes, products and services. They argue that it is now time to reconsider the IT role to be aligned or subordinated with business strategy. However, they identified four main elements to guide the concept of digital business thinking and to help to propose a framework for next-generation insight. These themes include: digital business strategy scope, digital business strategy scale, strategy speed and sources of value creation and detention in digital business strategy. They believe that these defined themes outline the key traits of digital business strategy and help to explain the role, nature and development of digital strategy in the context of next-generation insight.

According to Nylén and Holmström (2015), digital technology creates difficult innovative challenges. There are examples of firms that have failed to address them suitably and suffered major losses. Therefore, the question of how digital innovation should be managed, or whether it can be perfectly managed at all, is raised. Nylén and Holmström (2015) have presented a managerial framework to support the firm in continuous improvement in managing digital innovation. This framework covers five basic areas: value proposition, user experience, skills, digital revolution scanning and innovativeness. The study noted that since each firm has its unique characteristics, the way through which each measure is deployed and operationalized may considerably vary. Modifying the framework, therefore, involves deciding whether to apply qualitative or quantitative measures. Digital technology, indeed, opens many ways of data capturing. For instance, in the product dimension, a firm may negotiate with customers to motivate them to share their ideas to gain insight about using and purchasing patterns. In environmental terms, firms need to explore how they can scrape or capture web data from technology websites to get intelligence on digital technology developments that support their current business intelligence practices. Moreover, the study showed that besides the number of factors identified in the framework, there are some other factors which influence the digital innovation efforts of firms, such as regulation and political policies which are also very important in the context of innovation.

Digital transformation has significant importance in today's dynamic business world with all its sectors. Due to the need for technology in logistics, such as efficiency, cost, sustainability and security, digital innovation is of utmost importance to remain competitive. To understand the forthcoming challenges in this area, it is necessary to evaluate the results of past technology developments and their influence on port operations. To address this issue, Heilig, Schwarze, and Voß (2017) provide a comprehensive analysis of digital transformation in seaports by identifying three generations and analyzing the stages of digital transformation in each generation. This analysis includes the identification of digital transformation level required in the past to redesign processes, to extend service variety and to form inter-organizational networks to gain competitive advantage, that is, in form of productivity, efficiency, cost and safety improvements.

Heilig, Schwarze, and Voß's study has highlighted the significance of adopting modernized technological tools, such as Interplay, local IT/IS and product adaptation, which can lead to successful competitive advantage for both individual and overall ports. This study has further highlighted the incremental growth stages of digital transformation. Therefore, it is essential to identify and evaluate new approaches that support shaping activities and strategies of ports and logistics.

Today's mangers have many opportunities to innovate. Due to the wide distribution of inexpensive digital infrastructures, all business professionals seem to have a giant's digital shoulder to stand on when developing and convincing management to adopt innovation model. With the rapid increase in innovative models, many digital businesses founded by firms like Threadless.com and Quirky. com have made it easy to be used by normal users and do not need professional skills. Therefore, even if the managers are professional in technology, they can be innovators because of the easy use of digital technology available in their firms. Certainly, the wider "design thinking" movement, which inspires conventional managers to bring the designer's ideas and methods to organizational problem solving and innovation, is encouraged by the increasing distribution of digital infrastructures and related technical knowledge. This implies, given the increased importance of digitization to organizational success, that almost all business professionals today have the opportunity or even the obligation to become a digital innovator in some form (Fichman, Dos Santos, & Zheng, 2014).

Development in digital technology offers a wide range of opportunities in developing products and service. Digital transformation has the potential of many service innovation, and therefore digitization of products can lead to the emergence of new product architecture.

For example, digital transformation will help health care organizations to achieve their overall aim of improving health and providing access to health care, lowering health care capital costs and improving productivity and clinician experience. Since the beginning of the information and communication revolution era, technology has resulted in incredible innovations in the health care industry, such as the digitization of patient records, which enables health care professionals to monitor their patients from a distance. Technological advancements over cloud security during recent years have changed the organizational perspectives on the cloud. Moreover, digital crime units are now able to track cybercrimes by using Big Data and analytics, sophisticated technology. Innovation in health care financing, delivery and technology has made many advancements in the health care industry, but the sector still faces significant challenges with the fast-growing worldwide population. Governments are, however, struggling to maintain the required funding rate for health care systems. However, digital transformation is not only about technology. It means leaders have to re-envision their business models and lead the effort in bringing various departments on board to embrace the change.

Companies which efficiently handle digital technology can imagine gaining success in one or more of three key areas: streamlined operations, better customer engagement and experiences, and new business models or lines of business. Although new innovative business models are dreamed of by every CEO, companies mostly view digital technology as a support to transform their operations or customer experience. The transformation of the business model is difficult and far less predominant. Despite increasing acknowledgment of the need for digital transformation, many companies fight to get clear business advantage from using new digital technologies. There is still lack of management temperament and the related skills and experience to understand how effective transformation through technology can be. Even companies where the efficiency of technology has been demonstrated by the leaders can run into troubles and face challenges with the implementation of new digital technologies. Today's evolving technologies, like mobile, social media, analytics devices, demand different approaches and skill sets than did earlier streams of transformative technology (Fitzgerald, Kruschwitz, Bonnet, & Welch, 2014).

According to Lyytinen, Yoo, and Boland Jr (2016), increased digitization of products and organizational processes offer new challenges with respect to understanding the product innovation process. It also unlocks new horizons for research in information systems. Lyytinen et al. (2016) argued that advancement in digital technologies improves innovation network connectivity through minimizing communication costs and expanding its scope. Moreover, the advanced digital transformation increases the speed of digital convergence, which enhances network knowledge, diversity, and integration. These technological advancements stretch the network of existing innovation through reorganizing control and growing the demand for knowledge management across space and time.

. It observes that businesses are lacking opportunities to open up innovation more effectively and rapidly because of legacy technology and historical misunderstandings about the role of IT departments.

Although it is very critical for IT to enable innovation, a number of businesses are limited in their capacity to derive and implement digital transformation. It's obvious that if IT departments could devote less time in "keeping the lights on", they could then give more time in value creation, increasing revenues and reducing costs.

As companies move toward digitally transforming their businesses, they need a fundamental infrastructure network which allows them to quickly innovate. It is believed that the network should become an innovation platform to deliver, develop and secure applications. This could be well achieved through network architecture implementation and open software-centric. Enterprises today are facing great challenges which are reflected in intense competition from mostly domestic markets as digital technology development changes the customer expectation and business model. It is necessary for firms to adopt technological change in their environment in order to compete in the market. Inclusive use of information communication tools assists companies to widen their product varieties and increases customers' experiences by finding better ways to satisfy their demands.

Kostić (2018) argued that all companies face the challenge of digital transformation. In a business environment with information as a basic resource and low entry barriers, businesses are confronted with changes in business models and strategies. The fact should not be ignored that large companies can be endangered by small, new startups or by innovative companies that may enter the market. It is also noted that digital transformation can impact change in market structure and market competition. Competitive pressure among companies operating in the digital environment is becoming intense.

Empirical research reveals that companies have high expectations of increased revenue and reduced costs from digitization. However, to achieve desired results, there is a need to invest in digital ventures, which can only be provided by only few firms. The introduction of digitization into enterprises is critical not only in fighting against competitors but also in simply surviving. Digital transformation, therefore, has become the central idea of business strategies and development for businesses of all sizes. It is a tool to achieve larger business results by adoption of new technologies. Moreover, digital transformation includes not only the introduction of new technology and a customization process for products/ services but also the optimization of business processes, redefinition of the business model and management of organizational change. Digital transformation involves use of new technology for business to transform itself into a digitized business model fully concerned with customer needs and market needs. Digitization basically influences small- and medium-size firms. However, the current industrial revolution phase allows advanced technologies to be used by companies of all sizes. It is important to note, however, that in this digitized economy, only the companies which instinctively respond to technological changes and turn them to strategic advantage will last. Those who missed out on opportunities will fail (Kostić, 2018).

The convergence to so-called SMAC technologies, that is, social, mobile, analytical and cloud computing has resulted in an unprecedented digitization wave which is currently fueling innovation in society and business. Since digitization is embracing all factors of professional and personal lives, it is gaining priority for policymakers and managers. This digitization wave is generating opportunities for the business and information system engineering (BISE) community to get involved in innovation research practices and to enhance the discipline's visibility. However, since researchers have investigated the emerging integration and exploitation of digital technologies over many decades, they kept considering it a new phenomenon (Legner et al., 2017).

Digital transformation is influencing the whole economy in a number of ways: emergence of new business models, modifying the innovation process and rapidly changing firms' activities. These transformations alter both challenges and opportunities for various players in the innovation ecosystem. But these transformations also highlight the argument regarding the link between innovative strategies and digital transformation. The findings from several have suggested several studies things which should be considered important in the context of digital transformation: education and training, strengthening capacities and soft skills for innovation and interdisciplinary research (Legner et al., 2017). In addition, innovation policy is the most crucial factor impacting digital transformation development.

The capability to digitally innovate the business is largely derived by a clearly defined digital strategy reinforced by managers who develop a culture to transform their organizations towards innovation thinking and practice. Therefore, the power of a digital transformation business strategy lies in its objectives and scope. Less digitally mature companies are inclined towards individual technologies and have decidedly operational strategies in focus, whereas most mature companies develop digital strategies with a view to transforming the business. Digitally mature companies are in a better position to take benefits from collaboration as well as they tend to use cross-functional teams to implement digital incentives. These companies use digital transformation to deal with business risks emerged from the collaborative work styles. Therefore, these companies encourage innovation with digital technologies more readily than the companies that are less digitally mature.

In general, the above literature review argues that digital transformation has become a well-known thought in today's dynamic business environment. The increasing connectivity of individuals, businesses and machines has altered market demand. For staying competitive and keeping up, businesses need to adjust themselves according to these demands through digitizing their operations and business models. There are number of success stories about companies that use digital technology to create amazing innovations. By using social media, mobile devices, cloud and analytics, companies are changing their way of doing businesses. As digital technology stretches into each and every business corner across the world, it is forming a new platform with new rules. Digital has already reformed the customer expectations through the way employees cooperate and the possible business models. Emerging technologies such as 3D printing, robotics, the IoT and augmented reality will shortly result in major business changes. However, everything will not different in this digital world. Research literature shows that big traditional companies can out-compete growing digital startups if they hold the digital environment and find ways to make it theirs. The uncertainty does not help digital transformation to success. Hence, there is a need to understand the business methods and finding the way to new digital opportunities under the uncertain circumstances of business.

Digital transformation also offers many new growth opportunities and even the possibility of expanding to new business areas. Therefore, companies should engage in innovation process, ensure customer engagement, creative thinking and employee empowerment a collective decision. Most of the businesses already have started to convert to digital transformation, as they understand that it cannot be postponed to tomorrow.

Diversity and future of innovation in service

Diversity is progressively at risk in the early 21st century. Often diversity is theorized across gender, ethnicity, sexual preference, socioeconomic status and professional credentials, among other categories of difference. These are important and relevant considerations, and yet they are incomplete. Diversity is an integral part of the culture in many countries around the world. Quotas for broad gender diversity have become law in numerous countries, such as Norway, France, India and Israel. Little is known about the economic and innovation consequences of a growing and diverse array of external stakeholders with competing interests, coupled with the growing diverse internal structures of firms. The causes and consequences of organizational diversity within firms are often the subjects of scholarly examination. The analysis of diversity in organizations is normally isolated to one type of diversity. However, there is a broader nature of diversity than a single dimension such as gender.

There are two main types of diversity: diversity in scope and diversity in levels. Diversity in scope reflects both characteristics that are inherent, such as age and gender, and diversity in characteristics that are chosen, such as the type of education and type of expertise (including the field of specialization, such as in hard sciences or social sciences and humanities). Diversity in levels reflects characteristics that are chosen, such as education level (such as education at the high school level, undergraduate level, master's level and doctoral level). In respect of their impact on innovation, diversity in scope and level should have differential impacts, as explained herein. As well, the value of diversity in education, specialization, technological skill and gender may depend on the industry characteristics in which a firm operates.

D. J. Cumming and Leung (2018) formulate a theory on the interplay between the scope and levels of broad diversity and innovation to generate three main insights. Results of their study were consistent with theories which imply that diversity (age, gender, type of expertise) facilitates innovation. Diversity facilitates innovation in industries with high-technology that are male-dominated. Moreover, they found that firms with greater diversity generate more value-enhancing innovations.

Service firms and industries, unlike construction, manufacturing and extractive (e.g., fisheries, agriculture forestry petroleum, mining, quarrying) firms and sectors, are involved in providing service products as their main function. The nature of service transformations has significant implications for innovation. As cited by Carlborg, Kindström, and Kowalkowski (2014), the transformation of information services was being done by using new IT 20 years ago, whereas in physical and human services, the focus of larger organizations was primarily on back-office applications. Human services sectors employed some specific innovations (e.g., medications and diagnostic apparatus for health services) and applied information technology in order to better capture and employ data on the circumstances and complexities of individuals. Physical services employed, however, processing technologies and motorized transport, used information technology in logistics and suffered from the self-service challenge, wherein consumers could get low-cost new equipment for the purpose of producing their own service functions more suitably. Various transformative activities include inputs of different materials and equipment and the application of diverse knowledge, skills and bases. Distinguishing knowledge bases, communities of practice and professions will impact the conduct and structure of innovation.

At first glance, diversity, innovation and ethnicity do not look as closely connected. However, in the last few years there has been increasing policy and research interest in the role of ethnic innovators. The international economy is generating an unprecedented demand for an open-minded and diversified workforce, whereas highly skilled workers are looking for opportunities to employ their human capital overseas with the aim to increase their experience and income. An innovation simply means to introduce something completely new in the firm's operations, obtained through analytical knowledge. The improvement in existing products or modifications in organizational arrangement of existing processes can also be regarded as an innovation. Technological advances primarily result from things which people do. In theory, there are potential links between organizational diversity and innovation. Prior work is consistent with the view that there are benefits to the diversity of scope on innovation and regional economic growth. The key intuition is that diversity in scope brings about a variety of perspectives as well as greater patience and an enhanced tolerance for failure, which in turn enables and encourages more innovative approaches to problem-solving (Florida, 2014).

Workplace diversity fosters an environment where all ideas are shared. When multiple backgrounds and perspectives are represented, and when leaders' value differences, all employees can feel comfortable sharing ideas and honest opinions. It's key for colleagues to have a safe space to share. Diverse team members with dissimilar experiences and worldviews will produce those products/services which replicate the communities they serve. With the growing diversity of our global community, it only makes sense to reflect it among the teams that work within them. Therefore, a majority of the research literature provides compelling evidence that diversity unlocks innovation and contributes to market growth.

Perhaps the greatest efforts in recent years, in part stimulated by policymakers and media, have been on the economic importance of gender diversity on corporate boards. Prior evidence has shown an impact of gender diversity on corporate financial performance results in term of radical innovation and fraud reduction. This finding is consistent with other theories and evidence that women make financial decisions in ways that are distinct from men (Chen, Leung, & Evans, 2015; Cumming, Leung, & Rui, 2015).

While it is well known that gender diversity is important for innovation and related economic outcomes, there is a comparative dearth of theory or evidence on intersecting diversity in scope in different ways to bring about organizational improvements that facilitate innovative outcomes and economic growth. Diversity in the scope of education may bring rise to further improvements in innovation by enabling new combinations of ideas and methods that bring about innovative outcomes.

To further elaborate on the intuition about diversity of scope and innovation, it is helpful to consider recent examples from the news and a recent working paper. Gompers, Mukharlyamov, Weisburst, and Xuan (2014) show that women venture capitalists considerably underperform compared to their male counterparts, and the reason for this underperformance is directly attributable to the lack of help from their male colleagues. Further, in a recent update to this work in 2017, the same authors show that male venture capitalists with daughters perform better than their male counterparts without daughters. This gender bias in venture capital was seen in a legal battle at one of the world's most well-known venture capital funds – Kleiner Perkins – where a female partner sued her partners over gender discrimination. More generally, many firms backed by venture capitalists, including perhaps the most famous of all – Google – have been faced with gender discrimination lawsuits in recent years.

While diversity in scope has the potential to facilitate innovation, diversity in levels has the potential to do exactly the opposite. Diversity in levels gives rise to a mismatch in ability and incomplete understanding among peers. Diversity in levels increases the possibility of conflict and resentment among the board. As such, there is a greater likelihood of inefficient budget allocation to R&D, for example, as different board members' knowledge and experience leads to different organization goals.

A quite recent study by Mayer, Warr, and Zhao (2018) finds that firms which take steps to promote diversity make themselves more innovative in terms of patents created, product innovations and citations of patents – that implies the relevant inventions are also employed for developing new technologies. The study further finds that corporate policies that encourage pro-diversity cultures, particularly handling of minorities and women, improve future innovation proficiency. However, this positive effect is found to be strong during the period of economic downturn and in the firms which are highly innovative, that depends highly on human capital, have wider growth opportunities compared to those who do not use their human capital optimistically. These pro-diversity policies are also helpful to enhance firm value through stimulating impact on innovation efficiency.

Procedural justice theory suggests that board diversity should reflect regional diversity (Young & Ghoshal, 2016). Regions that have higher numbers of females should have more females on boards. Regions with more technological and physical science graduates should have greater proportions of such graduates on boards. Regions with greater numbers of social science graduates should have greater proportions of social scientists on boards. If boards deviate from their demographic characteristics, then such a deviation reflects biased appointments and exacerbated costs associated with poorly constructed boards. In turn, attention of board members is drawn to lobbying and rent seeking activity and a corporate culture where reward is not based purely on achievement. Related work has demonstrated that the diversity performance relation is stronger in achievement-based settings (Nederveen Pieterse, van Knippenberg, & van Dierendonck, 2013.). If an organization's diversity reflects regional demographic diversity, there is a greater likelihood that there will be less pronounced agency problems within the organization. This diversity pertains to characteristics that are a matter of scope, including the type of education and expertise, as well as gender.

The literature has also highlighted that recently there are more women holding leadership positions in business. The female leader shave represented more ethnically and racially diverse decision-makers which successful that business in term of higher the profits. Countless studies have shown that diversity has an immense impact on complex organizations. BCG's recent 2017 study of 171 Swiss, German and Austrian companies shows that companies which have highly gender-diverse boards generated approximately 34% of revenues from newly invented products and services in a recent three-year period. This compares with 25% revenue from innovation of companies which have the least gender diversity. The evidence from this study also suggests that the percentage of the upper-level female managers is positively linked with disruptive innovation, wherein a new business model, product or service fully changes the previously existing version (e.g., what video streaming has done to DVD rental stores and the transformation of traditional brick-and-mortar stores to online retail).

A team that is valued for its diversity shares a broader range of ideas and perspectives. When a company makes space for diverse voices and experiences, it makes space for innovative thinking. Cutting-edge business leaders already know that diverse teams produce innovative strategies and excellent customer experiences that generate higher revenues and profits. With time, most business leaders will invest in significant levels of diversity in their organizations because of the tangible business advantages.

With reference to cultural diversity and innovation, some research studies have revealed a moderately positive correlation between innovation and cultural diversity, identifying that cultural diversity has a greater influence on innovation when compared to other diversity indicators such as gender or age. For instance, according to Ozgen, Nijkamp, and Poot (2013), cultural diversity offers valuable opportunities. There are several positive effects of cultural diversity on the firm's innovation that work at the firm level and at the local community level. In addition to knowledge spillovers from practices and ideas, cultural diversity also helps to trade facilitation through trust, networks and institutional knowledge. Furthermore, immigrants may be self-selected positively in terms of creativity, intelligence, entrepreneurship and willingness to take risks. They may also assist in reducing positions of key personnel. In addition to this, mostly they are relatively young, which increases creativity and mobility. Their flexibility may improve decision-making in uncertain situations. These findings were also reconfirmed by the same authors in their late study (Ozgen, Nijkamp, & Poot, 2017).

There are several possible explanations for why cultural diversity increases the innovative power of companies and regions. Employees with varied backgrounds have explicit cultural knowledge that they use in examining and solving problems in different methods. Moreover, they are often more willing to take risks. Culturally diverse workforces, however, also pose challenges. These include language barriers and the possibility of conflict since different cultural values or methods of interpretation can lead to misunderstandings that, at least initially, make cooperating more difficult. Another key finding is that the diversity of an organization's teams also plays a crucial role: The more varied a team's members are in terms of their countries of origin, the more positive the impact on its ability to innovate.

Previous studies have debated that teams of persons with varied backgrounds are more efficient and capable of processing the business information and in making deeper utilization of information, which is essential to perform multifaceted tasks. However, Mohammadi, Broström, and Franzoni (2017) proposed that this argument can be further extended to the aggregate workforce level in high-technology firms. Generally, they argue that higher education and ethnic workforce diversity is associated with higher performance in radical innovation. This study validates that increased workforce diversity in both educational disciplinary and ethnic background is directly associated with a firm's turnover share created by drastic innovation. Although, more exterior collaborations seem to decrease the significance for educational diversity, the effect of ethnic diversity is, however, not influenced by external cooperation. These research findings have substantial and practical implications. The authors further recommend that companies may follow recruitment policies stimulated by greater disciplinary and ethnic diversity as a mode to lift the organizational innovativeness.

Literature on innovation management has revealed that innovation is strongly affected by the gender configuration of the R&D workforce, as it defines the pool of ideas as well as the way to interact with these ideas to develop new knowledge. In consequence, the relationship between innovation and employees' gender diversity is gradually being explored in pragmatic studies. Research studies on the relationship between innovation and gender diversity have been characterized through the presence of competing theories. Theories envisaging positive connotations have focused on three elements; retaining and attracting skilled workers, improving creativity and organizational learning, and servicing an increasingly diverse market. The contribution of gender diversity to innovation as creativity develops from the incorporation of conflicting views and perspectives. As knowledge, perspectives, life experiences and management skills of women and men vary, as does the level of competition and risk aversion, diversity in gender brings together various backgrounds which encourage innovation (Fernández, 2015).

Theories envisaging negative associations highlight that diverse gendered teams may construct social identity groups (women and men) where individuals collaborate with the members of other group but do not cooperate with members from another identity. Therefore, gender diversity is perceived to decrease intra-organizational cooperation, since social interaction is a result of sharing similar attributes across members. In this sense, diversity in gender can have negative significances for innovation. However, if it is assumed that individuals are more likely to have contacts with people from similar gender, the diversity in gender may also help to improve network collaboration with individuals outside the organization.

In general, research literature argue that top leaders make consistent decisions with their individual as well as collective cognitive structures, which are basically a function of their functional background, education and values and experience. These cognitive frames are created from experience, education and their interaction with others. However, the downside of these cognitive frames is that they reveal a high rigidity level. Therefore, it is often claimed that composition of top management team may directly influence innovation strategy and the outcomes of resulting innovation. In fact, there are some studies which suggest the positive relationship between the team members' diversity, task and creativity and reflexivity and information sharing which leads to performance outcomes and strong innovation.

However, some research studies had mixed findings in the examination of the relationship between innovation and diversity and innovation through a series of empirical measures. For instance, Østergaard, Timmermans, and Kristinsson (2011) stated that an econometric analysis identifies a positive link between diversity in gender and education on the possibility of innovation, but they also found a negative impact of age diversity and no significant impact of ethnicity on a firm's ability to innovate.

The world and our organizations are becoming more complex. With technology increasingly impacting every aspect of our personal and professional lives, what worked in management in the past does not work anymore. One theme that emerges in this context is the link between innovation and diversity. Many would argue that we now operate in an environment where we need people who think differently, bring different backgrounds and experiences, and approach problems from very different angles. In this context, one might argue that diversity ultimately forms the backbone of innovation and resilience in the time of change. And while there's more to diversity than just gender, it is a large part of the equation.

In order to endorse workforce diversity and make better use of diversity's ability to guarantee innovative power, the contemporary research literature recommends that small and mid-size enterprises, in particular, introduce diversity management measures which take cultural diversity into account, in addition to gender, age, sexual orientation and disabilities. Since resources are limited, communities and regions could play an important role here. Especially promising are multifaceted approaches that combine efforts to promote economic activity, community development and the education and training of potential employees, while also involving actors from business, the policy sphere, public administration and civil society. Mid-size companies, in particular, would benefit if such activities were coordinated on a regional level, facilitating an exchange of experience.

The future of innovation is therefore highly dependent on our ability to step into the collective experience and creativity of all participants in our ecosystem. Diversity results in innovation, and innovation is all about people who have their own passions. Every great achievement in this world has been accomplished by people who were passionate about something. Before an organization can become the next innovative leader, it must completely understand its own ecosystems, innovation architecture and innovation archetypes, as well as their own people and their professional and social behaviors, thinking styles, and interests and passions. By understanding company's innovation desire, needs and characteristics, management innovators can attain a holistic viewpoint of identifying the actions deeds foster innovative culture.

Manufacturing and future of innovation in service

Innovation basically means introducing something new. However, in a business context, innovation is considered and counted only when it is commercialized and publicly introduced. Innovation in the manufacturing sector covers an extensive range of fields such as introducing new product/processes, new equipment/technology, new material and so on. Businesses can opt to innovate for many reasons. The innovation approach could either be reactive or proactive. The main objective of such innovation can be to minimize the turnaround time, improve the product quality, reduce cost of production, attain the flexibility of customizing the product as per customer demands and gain other benefits that result in better product competitiveness. Management innovation is a change introduced in a management principle to improve any area of business activity.

The manufacturing sector all over the world has experienced an unrestrained decade: large developing countries have jumped into the first level of manufacturing countries. Despite severe recession upsetting the demand, as well as increasingly falling employment in advanced economies, manufacturing still has remained critically significant for both developing and developed economies. For developing nation, it continues to offer a way from existence agriculture to increasing profits and living standards. For advanced nations, it remains a vital source of competitiveness, innovation, immense contributions to exports, R&D and productivity growth. However, the manufacturing sector has now transformed – taking both challenges and opportunities – and neither policymakers nor business leaders can depend on past responses for the new manufacturing environment.

The manufacturing sector significantly contributes to the national economy, including exports. Its broad and far-reaching contribution involves gross domestic products, high investment returns, high paying jobs, exports, the strong relationship between manufacturing, science, innovation, engineering, technology and national security. However, it is critical that the general public and policymakers understand the influence of manufacturing innovation on society, economy and the economic portfolio of the country.

Global manufacturers face increased challenges and competitive pressure from low-cost manufacturers in the developing nations, increasingly changing customer demands, high product complexities and legal requirements. Intense competition in the global business world requires manufacturing firms to constantly develop their manufacturing operations for greater speed and efficiency. Moreover, in a rapidly changing business environment, it is difficult for manufacturing functions to maintain the operational competitive advantage with moderate speed improvement. The manufacturing functions must be capable of accepting large-scale improvements of an innovative and radical nature as a supplement to incremental enhancements. Schrettle (2013) highlights three different features of the new manufacturing process technology which help the firms to gain superior manufacturing capabilities through innovative production processes.

Firstly, understanding the investment strategy and adoption process of manufacturing technology can help to improve management capabilities related to process technology. Secondly, sustainability management is an important function of process innovation. Manufacturing firms are affected by the energy cost, especially in energy-intensive industries like metals manufacturing and chemicals manufacturing. Managers are forced by increased government regulation to reform their business models and hence are a major determinant for investments in green products and technologies. Thirdly, the timing of technology adoption in process management is also important for increasing firm performance. It shows that as early as investment in improving process as greater innovation is. However, the research literature does not provide any supportive insights in this area. The literature has comprehensively addressed the impact of timing on innovation in the manufacturing industry not only in the service industry. Issues addressed were the key issues in manufacturing firms that deal with optimization processes of operational performance, and for the top managers who develop business and technology strategy for the firm but not in service industry firms.

Yamamoto and Bellgran (2013) discussed the innovative features in manufacturing processes which are commonly known as a manufacturing process innovation (MPI). An MPI involves a number of activities, including technological advancements such as installing new equipment or adopting new technologies at factories. Another MPI may comprise changing information and material inflow, changing work processes or changing organizational behavior patterns within the organization. This study has focused on many different types of MPIs, including process or product innovation, technical or administrative innovation and production, marketing or management innovation. These different MPI types may need preconditions and different approaches for an organization to gain expected outcomes. Although many other studies have demonstrated innovation typologies in literature, they have not addressed the various MPI types nor discussed preconditions and approaches to attain different MPI types. Yamamoto and Bellgran (2013) found that different MPI types can be helpful to discuss managerial issues relevant to each type of MPI, and his proposed MPI model assists in explaining several MPI types in more structural form.

Researchers have characterized innovative manufacturing companies in ascending order of adopters, adapters and inventors to evaluate the factor inspiring these activities. In the case of small-size firms, adoption and creation were significantly related to research and development engagement, export orientation, technological advancement from parent establishments, receiving technological assistance from external agencies and providing parts to multinationals. For medium-size manufacturing companies, collaborative research, R&D support and adopting technology from patent companies are significant in innovating activities. However, adoption in small firms is related to export exposure and long-term operations. Collaborative research, R&D incentives and transfer of technology from patent companies were not significantly related to technology adoption in medium-size manufacturing firms (Hosseini & Narayanan, 2014).

Digitization of manufacturing has transformed the way companies produce products while digitization of services has transformed consumers' behavior and demands control. This change is so convincing that it is known as Industrial revolution 4.0, or the fourth industrial revolution. The first industrial revolution was characterized with steam machinates. The second revolution was characterized by mass production and assembly line using electricity. The third revolution was the adoption of computers that was the introduction of the smart systems using data and machine learning characterize the current fourth revolution.

Big Data management, utilizing digital technologies to connect the complete value chain process, the digitization of logistics and manufacturing, the growth of cyber-physical systems which enable collecting Big Data, applying IoT to putting other machines in communication with each other are some very important attributes of this new industrial revolution. This has made the service industry a huge facilitator to the manufacturing industry. For example, the network that creates communication between virtual reality and physical reality is a term of service that helps products and machines communicate with each other,

The manufacturing revolution started in 2011 when the Government of Germany encouraged the initiative of Industry 4.0 in collaboration with the scientific and industrial organization. The development of industrial change and gaining of a leadership role in the manufacturing sector of the world were key basic goals of the country. Meanwhile, a re-industrialization plan called the Advanced Manufacturing Partnership was developed by the United States which was intended for manufacturing innovation through adapting advanced smart machine learning system to foster the production. Similar to the US's project, France launched the "Alliance for Industry of the Future" in order to apply the digitization method for support innovation. Moreover, Japan has also implemented Society 5.0. Korea has also initiated its Manufacturing Innovation Plan. Intelligent manufacturing development has been emerging as a significant measure to create a competitive advantage for the manufacturing companies in major countries across the world. The Made in China Plan 2025, previously known as China Manufacturing 2025, is specifically aimed at promoting intelligent manufacturing with a special focus on the comprehensive integration of advanced information technology in the manufacturing industry (Baldassarre, Ricciardi, & Campo, 2017).

It is observed that all these initiatives are manufacturing focused initiatives to use the advanced digitization revolution in improving the production of goods. Since digitization is basically a service industry, the future of industry will be depending on service industry innovation.

The 4th industrial revolution is categorized by introducing concepts of "Internet of Things" and the "Internet of Service" into the manufacturing sector, which enable smart manufacturing with a horizontally or vertically joined production system. The term smart manufacturing has been coined by many agencies in the United States, such as NIST (National Institute of Standards and Technology) and DoE (Department of Energy). The smart manufacturing concept involves the use digitized technology and the services of data analytics in order to enhance manufacturing processes. Randhawa & Sethi (2017) have discussed the concept of smart manufacturing in terms of accelerating innovation and improving the productivity of the firm. The big data analysis shows that a key factor of smart manufacturing is performance metrics. The influential internet availability of information and data related to manufacturing process opens untouched opportunities for increasing manufacturing innovation and productivity. Smart manufacturing offers a standard protocol for building internet simulation, modeling and data analytic tools which put manufacturing related internet data into working form. Another recent study by Thoben, Wiesner, and Wuest (2017), has focused on the fourth industrial revolution, comprised of Industry 4.0 and smart manufacturing. The researchers highlight the fast paradigm shift which manufacturing research and manufacturing industries are experiencing today. Smart manufacturing and Industry 4.0 demonstrate the transition towards highly focused data, increased automation and supply network-wide assimilation of communication and technology. Their objectives are diverse and multiple, with sustainability energy savings, resilience/agility and efficiency, and quality improvement being the central objective. Moreover, the study suggests that due to already available successful test beds, smart manufacturing and Industry 4.0 are still in their beginning phase. Therefore, increased attention and contributions from funding agencies as well as high industry interest can result in rapid growth in this field in the near future. The study found that smart manufacturing is highly responsive to innovation-oriented production and performance improvement. It was identified that considerable innovation has been gained in recent years in information and communications technology. These innovations allow the placement of distributed and real-time embedded computing systems which can be converted into key elements of smart manufacturing development.

Though innovation has gained significant importance for companies, getting consistent innovation capability poses high challenges to managers. Many recent studies have focused on large companies in order to examine their experience in constructing an effective team for the purpose of innovation management activities. Bagno, Salerno, and Dias (2017) observed innovation as an emerging and distinct organizational function and examined the characteristics of this function in large manufacturing companies. Their analysis identified the characteristics of innovation function in six perspectives, including legitimacy and guidance, origins, general purpose, assignments, people and future perspectives. This categorization of innovation functions adds new value to existing information about companies to develop and maintain a systemic and regular innovation capability. The basic aim of this innovation function is to catalyze the happening of innovation function and in order to this, this function involves a team of specialists to interrelate with other organizational parts.

In the context of innovation management, innovation function is used as a new unit of analysis. The use of innovation performance to indicate the industrial performance leads to offering new insights and perspectives to extend the understanding of innovation function and its characteristics.

There are a number of research studies which have focused on intelligence manufacturing in the context of software, hardware, robotics, additive manufacturing and Industry 4.0, but recently, Wang (2018) provided a different view by investigating related challenges and giving examples of some less touched but important topics, such as redefining advance manufacturing, hybrid system, ecosystem readiness, basic building blocks and technology scalability. One of the key major challenges identified by trends of the future of manufacturing. The trends imply that if a company wishes to increase public awareness about new manufacturing societal and economic effects and gathers the clear assistance of policymakers and should be aligned with the service industry innovation and development. Another big challenge is to identify that future manufacturing will be comprised of a hybrid system of a robotic and human operator, metal and composite material, subtractive and additive processes, and physical and cyber system. All are under the influence of the services and service innovation represented in the services of analysis, big data utilization, and customer satisfaction with the added value services. Moreover, developing a common framework wherein manufacturing business cases, ecosystem readiness and technology can be evaluated concurrently to reduce the time products take to reach customers will be difficult as the services systems have higher impacts on customers' perceptions and expectations.

Recently, increased attention has been focused on the idea of "Open Innovation", both on an academic and practical level. The "Open Innovation" term was coined by Chesbrough, who describes the concept in his book, *Open Innovation: The New Imperative for Creating and Profiting from Technology*. One of the new ways to innovate is for companies to switch their innovation systems towards openness by considering and taking into account the external resources of innovation. Conventionally, marketing and business development processes of new products occurred within the boundaries of the firm. However, a large number of factors have resulted in the destruction of closed innovation processes.

Availability and mobility and availability of highly skilled and educated people have considerably increased over the last few years. Consequently, an extensive body of knowledge exists for large companies external to their research laboratories. Moreover, when employees switch their jobs, they take with them their skills and knowledge, resulting in the flow of knowledge among firms. Secondly, there has been increased accessibility of venture capital in the last few years which offers the further development of technology and promising ideas outside the firm. In addition to the potentials to further developed technologies and ideas external to the firm, for example, in the shape of spin-offs or by licensing agreements, are increasing. Finally, some other supply chain companies such as suppliers have a vital role to play in the process of innovation. Consequently, companies have now started to search for other ways to improve the efficiency and productivity in their innovation developments, such as through actively searching for new ideas and technologies outside of the firm and also seeking assistance from cooperating competitors and suppliers in the creation of added customer value. An additional important feature is to further develop the out-licensing of technologies. Open

Innovation, therefore can be defined as combining the external and the internal resources of ideas to develop or enhance services, goods, offering and markets.

In the last few years, the open innovation concept has increasingly been highlighted by scholars in the context of manufacturing companies. Recently, Von Krogh, Netland, and Wörter (2018) addressed the topic of open innovation in terms of process innovation in manufacturing companies. The research notes that manufacturers are substantially benefited when they search ideas outside the factory, particularly when they already have advanced business operations.

Mostly, managers of manufacturing companies tightly preserve process innovation activities. Some view their processes as a source of their competitive advantage, and therefore they should not be disclosed or shared. Some others consider process innovation as organizational knowledge which could be harmful to the business if disclosed to outsiders. However, few companies have good motives behind concealing their innovation processes. For instance, a combination of product and process innovation often together results in gaining competitive advantage.

In the manufacturing sector, SMEs, that is, small-to-medium enterprises, make major contributions to economic development, but the majority of research on innovation management in the context of the manufacturing sector has been focused on large manufacturing organizations. However, Brunswicker, and Vanhaverbeke (2015) explored the open innovation in medium- and small-size manufacturing companies. This study investigated how small- and medium-size manufacturing companies use external knowledge sources and facilitate the internal to manage innovation. It empirically theorizes the typology of outside knowledge sourcing which describes the distinct types of openness strategies. These strategies assist the small-and-medium enterprises (SMEs) in having an opportunity to enhance their innovation performance as well as to relate to a discrete set of internal practices to manage innovation. The study concluded that openness in small-and-medium companies is dependent on their inter-organizational association for innovation. They mostly are lacking in capacity to purposively making use of these links for new knowledge and ideas in innovation. Results, however, suggest that small-and-medium enterprises are engaged in innovation through sourcing of purposive external knowledge.

Practitioners and scholars have jointly agreed on the fact that service innovation is critical for companies looking for a place in the industry that will ensure survival over the long run. They state that in a rapidly changing business environment, firms can only compete through diverse intangible resources such as innovative skills which are expected to be valuable, rare and imperfectly capable. Since it is perceived as a vehicle of economic development, it is possible for service innovation to be the source of enhancement of firm performance in all other non-service sectors.

Therefore, an inquiry of factors which impact the innovation process should be a managerial and academic concern. To address this issue, Kamasak (2015) conducted a study to investigate the key determinants of innovation to enhance innovation performance. According to this study, innovation strategy, technological capabilities and innovation culture are strongly linked with innovation performance. This implies that technological capabilities such as electronic data interchange (EDI), supply chain management (SCM), enterprise resource planning (ERP) and electronic data interchange (EDI) enable the companies to get sufficient intelligence relating to existing and future needs, channel requirements, competitors' action and strategies, and wider business environment. The study, however, found technological capabilities and innovation strategy as key drivers for firms innovation performance. The study has also found that firms need to restructure their technology resources to improve their service innovation.

Rapidly increasing competition in the international and domestic market simply means that companies cannot maintain cost advantage over the long run. It has been experienced by the successful worldwide companies that organizational success depends on a continuous process of innovation, so in order to win a good position in the competition race, businesses can innovate on several aspects of processes, manufacturing, management principles and technology. Innovation is not only a one-time practice; rather it involves nonstop efforts in re-inventing the products, processes and the services in term of technology and market developments. Therefore, firms need to develop specialized teams, specific strategies and performance metrics. One of the major drivers of manufacturing innovation is technological advancement. Gaining technological advancements can help manufacturers in creating high-quality goods in a shorter time frame than before. This in turn will lead to create highly efficient operations and strong competitive strategy. However, a manufacturer can also be innovative in many other ways beyond the technology use. Innovation, therefore, can also include the utilizing of new business models, new processes/services development as well as the development of existing products. The quality of the workforce's skills will be the critical factor in gaining competitive advantage. It is therefore essential for policymakers to focus on supplying a skilled workforce, including training schemes, support to researchers and supplying skilled managers. The firm will also need to give more attention to structuring multidisciplinary teams in order to develop highly complex products and advanced business models.

To conclude, the future of manufacturing is going to depend on service offerings that add to the goods to gain more value. Through digitization, the pace of servitization will increase to completely dominate goods offering and control customers' demands, satisfaction level and expectation.

Environment and sustainability and the future of service innovation

Environmental and sustainability issues are increasingly emerging as a significant topic for management, manufacturing, strategic business and product development decisions. Awareness of the nature and environment motivated producers and service providers to green and seek developing environment friendly products and services. The purpose of the firm to develop sustainable programs is to green their products and processes while minimizing the influence of their activities. In order to eradicate the problems related to environmental pollution, eco-friendly management concepts, like green marketing, green production, green innovation, green management and so on are currently being widely pursued.

Sustainability has gradually become significant to business research and processes in recent decades due to speedy natural resources depletion and concerns related to corporate social responsibility. The term sustainability has been defined as the firm's ability to meet the current needs without compromising on the ability of future generation to satisfy their needs. This definition can be drawn back to the Brundtland Report published in 1987 and later to Rio de Janeiro Earth Summit in 1992 and the Johannesburg Summit in 2002, where environmental and sustainability issues gained increased attention "to become one of the leading issues facing by the world".

Perceptions have been developed which outline sustainability through three mechanisms: the natural environment, economic performance and social performance. Generally, this perspective is referred to as TBL, that is, Triple bottom line. These three dimensions generally are accepted as an explanation for sustainable performance of a company. The environmental performance has been defined as the "outcome of environmental aspects from an organization's management" (Morrow & Rondinelli, 2002). Environmental performance, therefore, focuses on the company's influence on living as well as non-living natural resources, including air, land, water and ecosystem.

Over the past two decades, many empirical studies in management science and economics have been conducted to consider service innovation as a legitimate, related, and emerging important subject in the area of innovation studies. To some extent, recent development in this research field is evidenced by an increasing number of both quantitative and qualitative literature reviews which have covered the subject of service innovation in both its specific and general aspects that related to environment green industries.

Recent empirical innovation studies have been supported in several ways the friendly environment innovation. The support have been by examining the new ideas of service innovation (e.g., social innovation, KIBS in innovation, public policies for service innovation, public-private innovation networks). Furthermore, in the last few years, there has been increased interest in the literature to empirically and theoretically investigate the evolving topic related to sustainable innovation. Many of these have studies focused on service innovation and its ability to be consistent with the current socioeconomic issues with regards to suitability and green industries. Hence, sustainability certainly has become a key issue in service industry and service innovation.

Existing economies are undoubtedly service economies and, in order to be sustainable economies, they should address the question of the relationship between sustainable development and services innovation. However, despite certain important exceptions like reporting of unfavorable effects of tourism and transport on the environment, little consideration was paid to this question yet. Therefore, sustainability is still perceived as a main industrial issue.

The current trends of environmental protection, sustainability and competitiveness has led to a new concept, namely, eco-innovation, which is a term rarely used so far. The reality indicates that certain forms of eco-innovation can be implemented in a simple way. Innovation must contribute to environmental performance and thus obtains eco-innovation connotations, something necessary given the current challenges faced by climate change, energy security, and natural resources. Besides these aspects, any organization following this concept finds eco-innovation as a lever to increase its competitiveness in the goods and industrial services market.

The term eco-innovation is relatively new. The first use was in 1996 by the Fussler (in the publication "Driving Eco-Innovation") with reference to new goods and processes which offer value to businesses and customers while significantly decreasing the environmental effect, showing a similar significance as the "environmental innovation", the "innovation for sustainable development" or the "sustainable innovation". Making an analogy with innovation, we can say that eco-innovation means the "modification of any product, service, process, organizational change, or marketing solution that helps reduce resource utilization and reduce the release of toxic substances throughout the life cycle" (Fussler, 1996).

The innovative services signify a new perception of services, considerably improved as compared to the traditional services concepts; it is progressively becoming common practice. Innovations in services may also result to bring changes in innovative factors in other business sectors and ultimately support the company's development. Prosperous services firms strive to remain competitive through innovative practices. They struggle because there is no doubt that the way by which a service is designed and delivered has a strong influence on consumer buying decision. In addition, they face challenges because of the intense competition in the market (Irina & Aniela, 2013).

Sustainability-oriented innovative practices are perceived to be a main resource of organizational sustainability. The challenge is how to make sustainability-oriented innovation produce improved products, services, processes and management systems. Previous literature and publications have widely argued the important issues related to integrated sustainability features into the process of innovation, yet there exists little empirical research which has focused on evaluating the connection between sustainable innovation and organizational performance overall. Corporate sustainability-related issues are increasingly gaining importance in the management literature research field, plus those related to corporate environmentalism (Kudłak, 2014). Organizations are challenged with social and environmental-related problems in their decisions, and they need not only to consider legal and moral responsibility but also to ensure successful sustainable development (Koo, Chung, & Ryoo, 2014).

Attaining environmental sustainability is a critical issue for the companies that are developing specific innovation which have favorable environmental outcomes, in order to incorporate the environment in their business strategies. Implementation of green innovation offers a big challenge to non-green companies because it mostly demands the new resource acquisition and competencies which significantly differ from their current competencies.

Previous studies on environment sustainability revealed that environmental management of an organization may strengthen their financial goals. Even if it cannot perhaps improve profitability in the short term, it could generate economic profits over the long term. One of the ways by which companies develop their strategies by integrating environmental issues while strengthening their competitive position is through innovations that can have positive environmental effects. In fact, it has been confirmed that the green innovations performance, both as processes or products, are positively associated with a business's competitive advantage.

Green innovation can be defined as "innovations process that comprises of new or revised practices, processes, products and systems which help the environment and result in environmental sustainability". It can further lead reducing inefficiencies as well as rational utilization of natural resources, creating an important source of cost reduction. However, on the other side, by considering the increased customer awareness about environmental influences of consumption choices, companies can use the environmental characteristics of new products/services in order to create marketing differentiation. Therefore, focus on green innovation management is increasingly becoming a hot topic both in academia and practice.

Researchers and policymakers such as OECD are becoming highly interested in sustainable innovation and organizational performance. Defining and understanding the concept of sustainable innovation and its dimensions is a difficult task, as some research has been done on this topic in several disciplines. Though one can accept the definition suggested by the research literature, such as:

> Sustainable innovation is a practice where sustainability attentions (such as economic social, and environmental) are combined into the system of the company from idea creation to R&D (research and development), and advertisement. This applies to technologies, products, services, as well as the innovative organization and business models.
>
> (OECD, 2005)

According to Klewitz and Hansen (2013), researchers' arguments on organizations, which struggle toward sustainable development goals from innovative practices, were primarily focused towards eco-innovations. The literature revealed that eco-innovation can be theorized by employing the following dimensions: product-service dimensions, user dimensions, governance dimensions design dimensions and the engagement of key stakeholder in the innovation process. However, the ultimate goal of putting efforts in eco-innovations is to offer new business opportunities as well as contributing towards a sustainable society.

Shafie, Siti-Nabiha, and Tan (2014) identified that the environment in which business operates is dynamic and gradually becoming highly competitive globally. Given the rapidly evolving and changing business environmental conditions, innovation has become a key foundation of sustainable competitive advantage. Therefore, Shafie et al. have proposed that organizations need to incessantly pursue advancements through involvement in innovation practices in order to remain profitable and competitive. However, the innovation could even fail if companies bring these into the market without brand association and necessary communication Shafie et al. further noted that quality top management teams (TMTs) can serve as a critical factor in influencing branding efforts and innovation. Issues related to TMTs are considered to be central in the company's innovation capability. For instance, some top managers would desire to maintain the status quo. Top management teams also specify that the difference between the innovation level they want for their firms and the innovation level achieved is large. This difference in innovation level is called the innovation gap. Shafie et al. also showed that no correlation was found between market share and the spending level R&D. In particular, some businesses are unsuccessful in addressing factors like corporate culture, corporate strategy, business models and firm's capability to commercialize their innovation. Addressing this innovation gap seems to be complex in nature; it needs further research to identify the relationship between innovation and firm sustainability.

Stamler (2016) has also contributed in the area of sustainable service innovation by addressing the relationship between economic sustainability and innovation. Stamler examined the relationship between brand, innovation and sustainable financial performance to examine the link between sustainability and innovation. The study found that the links between sustainability, brand and innovation are related to top management teams who should balance long-term goals and short-term goals, considering that innovation involves careful decision-making to reap quick financial gain or to invest in undefined future opportunities.

Maletič, Maletič, Dahlgaard, Dahlgaard-Park, and Gomišček (2016) found in their research study that organizations are benefited from incorporating sustainability aspects in their business products and operations. To some extent, these findings are consistent with the previous literature, which stated that including sustainability activities in process and product development can help companies improve their economic benefits through tools and mechanisms without influencing communities and environment. Moreover, the findings of this study proposed that innovation-related competencies have a major role in organizational performance. These findings are consistent with a number of prior studies that have discussed the significance of sustainability learning in relation to sustainable innovation and ultimately resulting in an efficient move to sustainability.

With reference to the impact of sustainable innovation practices on innovative performance, this research study has also made an important contribution to the previous literature and proposed that involvement in sustainability engagement drives innovations Furthermore, an organization's innovativeness can also be influenced by stakeholders' engagement which is perceived as a significant organizational capability.

Regional developers and national innovation systems both are striving to meet the constantly changing demands from the highly competitive global environment. Cities, regions and countries all across the world experience structural changes due to the shift of the economy from manufacturing to services and due to landscape innovation due to socio-technical development. Therefore, there is a need to develop and strengthen the local innovation environment to efficiently support the innovation and to manage the structural change.

The research literature also recommends that top management focus on building innovative competencies which are assumed as a key device essential to understand and maximize the impact of sustainability development on an organization's performance. For this purpose, the organization's ability to create sustainable and innovative solutions (e.g., process and product innovations, and innovations in services) can be considered as an organizational resource. Managers must therefore develop an effective mechanism to sustain these resources and utilizing them effectively to improve their performance as well as to gain competitive advantage. Consequently, managers should struggle to gain excellence in sustainable innovation as the ability to develop innovative products/services in such a way which could satisfy the customers and other stakeholders (such as suppliers, employees, society) over the short term as well as in the long run in balanced way. Therefore, managers who emphasis value creation over the long run may be well guided to direct resources for the purpose of increasing both innovativeness and sustainability performance.

In business firms, innovation has been inspired by the need to create superior competitive position in the marketplace. Traditionally, it has been successfully achieved from two basic strategies: cost cutting or product differentiation through making products superior to their competitors. However, sustainable innovation provides the third competitive advantage in creating products, services or processes with highly desirable market features such as locality, durability or energy and material efficiency.

The significance of the service sector has received increasing attention in the last three decades since services represent most of the GDP in many developed nations, and even economies which traditionally focused on manufacturing have been rapidly growing in services. In the meantime, service innovation has been considered as "the next big thing", but a number of research studies based on innovation still have focused on innovation in manufacturing sector. There is a shortage of empirical studies discussing the differences between manufacturing innovation and services innovation as well as to address service innovation and new service growth activities.

One of the service innovation research trends that indicates the future of service innovation is the sustainability in Asia. There has been a numerous industrial growth and service revolution in most of Asian countries. This growth has raise sustainability awareness in Asia more than the rest of the world. Eco-consciousness scholars have argued the effect of commercial technology and outdated traditional production systems on sustainability and environment in Asian countries (Tseng, Tan, & Siriban-Manalang, 2013). Some scholars believe that the innovation process is effective to achieve sustainable development. A business needs incomes for production of product, consumers demand high-quality products at inexpensive price, whereas society demands a safe environment free from pollution for the generations that follow (Chou, Horng, Liu, Huang, & Chung, 2016). Unfortunately, protecting the environment has not been that easy, because the anticipated outcomes of green innovation are hard to achieve if government, society and industry do not cooperate and work jointly on eco-innovations.

On the basis of prior studies on eco-innovation, scholars have identified that eco-innovation is not applicable to all implementation levels, as implementation and level of implementation is itself dependent on the innovation type. They suggest that an investigation of different attributes of sectors and firms may help to better explain the eco-innovation practices and its effective implementation. However, it is critical to evaluate the effect of eco-innovation on results from sustainable business performance. The company's sustainability must address the opportunities and challenges offered by eco issues. A firm can be able to add service values to its customers by involving in service innovation. However, one of the best ways to effective service innovation implementation for a firm could be continuously seeking possibilities through understanding and learning their businesses.

Current social, economic and environmental sustainability challenges gradually are becoming a motivation source for both service and manufacturing companies. In the last few years, increased interest from practitioners, academics and policymakers on the topic of service innovation has raised a new concept for companies to use when they answer societal challenges related to sustainability and innovation. However, research specifically addressing the service innovation related to sustainability is rare and eventually spread across diverse research fields. Thus, only limited evidence is available for a company willing to attempt sustainability challenges through the process of service innovation.

As environmental concern has got attention from the public and scholars as well, the innovation has been significantly recognized in the discussion of sustainability. However, empirical evidence suggests that an innovation resulting from environmental factors produces the same success in the context of cost savings and cost as a regular innovation would produce, maybe because "eco-innovators are able to derive profit from lesser innovation uncertainty due to regulatory controlling standards as well as demand-generating impact of these regulation". Regulation plays an improved role in the sustainability innovation. On the other side, sustainability and regulation alone are not sufficient. Pragmatic studies in Finland identified that common sustainability projects without a specific innovative aspect fail to create new business, leaving idle a big part of company's capacity to enhance sustainability.

To encourage additional research in this field, (Calabrese, Castaldi, Forte, & Levialdi, 2018) have recently studied the existing literature through exploring peer-reviewed publications for the period between 2004 and 2015 through different areas, which equally emphasize service, sustainability and innovation. Moreover, the literature also exposed that three key existing research areas (product-service system, service innovation and sustainable innovation) mainly contribute to the research topic. Although all have specific focus on innovation and sustainability dimensions, examining thematic and descriptive analysis of evaluation and the research gaps identified, Calabrese et al. (2018) conclude that there is still a need to clearly recognize the evolving field of sustainable service innovation and fill the gap through further enhancement.

In general, discussion about the nature and sustainable development has gained significant importance. This could be helpful in achieving future requirements to gain environment-friendly service innovation and goods innovation. In organizations, innovation process is linked to organizational sales, external environment and innovation culture that perceived environment, sustainability and green industries.

References

Agnete Alsos, G., Ljunggren, E., & Hytti, U. (2013). Gender and innovation: State of the art and a research agenda. *International Journal of Gender and Entrepreneurship, 5*(3). https://doi.org/10.1108/IJGE-06-2013-0049

Auriga. (2016). *Digital transformation: History, present, and future trends.* Retrieved from Https://Auriga.Com/Blog/2016/Digital-Transformation-History-Present-and-Future-Trends/

Bagno, R. B., Salerno, M. S., & Dias, A. V. C. (2017). Innovation as a new organizational function: Evidence and characterization from large industrial companies in Brazil. *Production, 27.*

Baldassarre, F., Ricciardi, F., & Campo, R. (2017). The Advent of Industry 4.0 in Manufacturing Industry: Literature Review and Growth Opportunities. In *DIEM: Dubrovnik International Economic Meeting* (Vol. 3, pp. 632–643). Sveučilište u Dubrovniku.

Bharadwaj, A., El Sawy, O., Pavlou, P., & Venkatraman, N. (2013). Digital business strategy: toward a next generation of insights. *MIS Quarterly, 37*(2), 471–482.

Brunswicker, S., & Vanhaverbeke, W. (2015). Open innovation in small and medium-sized enterprises (SMEs): External knowledge sourcing strategies and internal organizational facilitators. *Journal of Small Business Management, 53*(4), 1241–1263.

Calabrese, A., Castaldi, C., Forte, G., & Levialdi, N. G. (2018). Sustainability-oriented Service Innovation: An emerging research field. *Journal of Cleaner Production, 193*, 533–548.

Carlborg, P., Kindström, D., & Kowalkowski, C. (2014). The evolution of service innovation research: A critical review and synthesis. *The Service Industries Journal, 34*(5), 373–398. https://doi.org/10.1080/02642069.2013.780044

Chen, J., Leung, W. S., & Evans, K. P. (2018). Board gender diversity, innovation and firm performance. *SSRN Electronic Journal, July.* Retrieved from https://papers.ssrn.com/sol3/papers.cfm?abstract_id=2607295

Chou, S.-F., Horng, J.-S., Liu, C.-H., Huang, Y.-C., & Chung, Y.-C. (2016). Expert concepts of sustainable service innovation in restaurants in Taiwan. *Sustainability, 8*(8), 739.

Cumming, D. J., & Leung, T. Y. (2018). Diversity and Innovation: The Differential Role of Scope Versus Levels. *SSRN Electronic Journal, May.* Retrieved from https://papers.ssrn.com/sol3/papers.cfm?abstract_id=3181323

Cumming, D., Leung, T. Y., & Rui, O. (2015). Gender diversity and securities fraud. *Academy of Management Journal, 58*(5), 1572–1593.

Eriksson, A. (2014). A gender perspective as trigger and facilitator of innovation. *International Journal of Gender and Entrepreneurship, 6*(2), 163–180.

Ernst, & Young. (2015). *Megatrends 2015: Making Sense of a World in Motion.* Retrieved from https://www.ey.com/Publication/vwLUAssets/ey-megatrends-report-2015/%24FILE/ey-megatrends-report-2015.pdf

Fernández, J. (2015). The impact of gender diversity in foreign subsidiaries' innovation outputs. *International Journal of Gender and Entrepreneurship, 7*(2), 148–167.

Fichman, R. G., Dos Santos, B. L., & Zheng, Z. E. (2014). Digital innovation as a fundamental and powerful concept in the information systems curriculum. *MIS Quarterly, 38*(2).

Fitzgerald, M., Kruschwitz, N., Bonnet, D., & Welch, M. (2014). Embracing digital technology: A new strategic imperative. *MIT Sloan Management Review, 55*(2), 1–12. Retrieved from https://search.proquest.com/docview/1475566392?accountid=30552

Florida, R. (2014). The link between religious diversity and economic development. *CityLab, December, 19.*

Foss, L., Moilanen, M., & Woll, K. (2013). Creativity and implementations of new ideas: Do organisational structure, work environment and gender matter? *International Journal of Gender and Entrepreneurship, 5*(3), 298–322. https://doi.org/10.1108/IJGE-09-2012-0049

Freeman, R. B. (2015). Who owns the robots rules the world. *IZA World of Labor.*

Fussler, C. (1996). Driving eco-innovation: A breakthrough discipline for innovation and sustainability. *Financial Times Management.*

Gompers, P. A., Mukharlyamov, V., Weisburst, E., & Xuan, Y. (2014). Gender effects in venture capital. *SSRN Electronic Journal.* Retrieved from https://ssrn.com/abstract=2445497 or http://dx.doi.org/10.2139/ssrn.2445497

Hădărean Ùomlea, I. N., Marian, L., & Ferencz, I. S. (2014). Customer satisfaction analysis by the implementation of Quality Management System in a public institution. *Procedia Economics and Finance, 15*, 1071–1076. https://doi.org/10.1016/S2212-5671

Hajkowicz, S. A., Reeson, A., Rudd, L., Bratanova, A., Hodgers, L., Mason, C., & Boughen, N. (2016). Tomorrow's digitally enabled workforce: Megatrends and scenarios for jobs and employment in Australia over the coming twenty years. *Australian Policy Online.*

Heilig, L., Schwarze, S., & Voß, S. (2017). An analysis of digital transformation in the history and future of modern ports. In *50th Hawaii International Conference on System Sciences* (pp. 1341–1350). Retrieved from https://scholarspace.manoa.hawaii.edu/bitstream/10125/41313/1/paper0164.pdf

Hosseini, S. M. P., & Narayanan, S. (2014). Adoption, adaptive innovation, and creative innovation among SMEs in Malaysian manufacturing. *Asian Economic Papers, 13*(2), 32–58.

Huyer, S. (2015). Is the gender gap narrowing in science and engineering. *UNESCO Science Report: Towards 2030, 85.*

Joensuu-Salo, S., & Sorama, K. (2016). Megatrends and innovations: A gender approach. In *Entrepreneurship, innovation and regional development (EIRD 2016) June 28–29, 2016: conference papers.* European Council for Small Business and Entrepreneurship.

Kamasak, R. (2015). Determinants of innovation performance: A resource-based study. *Procedia-Social and Behavioral Sciences, 195*, 1330–1337.

Klewitz, J., & Hansen, E. G. (2014). Sustainability-oriented innovation of SMEs: A systematic review. *Journal of Cleaner Production, 65,* 57–75.

Koo, C., Chung, N., & Ryoo, S. Y. (2014). How does ecological responsibility affect manufacturing firms' environmental and economic performance? *Total Quality Management & Business Excellence, 25*(9–10), 1171–1189.

Kostić, Z. (2018). Innovations and digital transformation as a competition catalyst. *Ekonomika, 64*(1), 13–23.

Kudłak, R. (2014). Critical insights from the corporate environmentalism–competitiveness investigations. *Management of Environmental Quality: An International Journal, 25*(2), 111–131.

Kvidal, T., & Ljunggren, E. (2014). Introducing gender in a policy programme: A multilevel analysis of an innovation policy programme. *Environment and Planning C: Government and Policy, 32*(1), 39–53.

Legner, C., Eymann, T., Hess, T., Matt, C., Böhmann, T., Drews, P., . . . Ahlemann, F. (2017). Digitalization: Opportunity and challenge for the business and information systems engineering community. *Business & Information Systems Engineering, 59*(4), 301–308.

Lyytinen, K., Yoo, Y., & Boland Jr, R. J. (2016). Digital product innovation within four classes of innovation networks. *Information Systems Journal, 26*(1), 47–75. https://doi.org/http://dx.doi.org/10.1111/isj.12093

Maletič, M., Maletič, D., Dahlgaard, J. J., Dahlgaard-Park, S. M., & Gomišček, B. (2016). Effect of sustainability-oriented innovation practices on the overall organisational performance: An empirical examination. *Total Quality Management & Business Excellence, 27*(9–10), 1171–1190.

Mayer, R. C., Warr, R. S., & Zhao, J. (2018). Do pro-diversity policies improve corporate innovation? *Financial Management, 47*(3), 617–650. https://doi.org/http://dx.doi.org/10.1111/fima.12205

Mazzone, D. M. (2014). *Digital or death: Digital transformation: The only choice for business to survive smash and conquer.* Smashbox Consulting Inc.

Mohammadi, A., Broström, A., & Franzoni, C. (2017). Workforce composition and innovation: How diversity in employees' ethnic and educational backgrounds facilitates firm-level innovativeness. *Journal of Product Innovation Management, 34*(4), 406–426.

Morrow, D., & Rondinelli, D. (2002). Adopting corporate environmental management systems: Motivations and results of ISO 14001 and EMAS certification. *European Management Journal, 20*(2), 159–171.

Nählinder, J., Tillmar, M., & Wigren, C. (2015). Towards a gender-aware understanding of innovation: A three-dimensional route. *International Journal of Gender and Entrepreneurship, 7*(1), 66–86.

Nederveen Pieterse, A., Van Knippenberg, D., & Van Dierendonck, D. (2013). Cultural diversity and team performance: The role of team member goal orientation. *Academy of Management Journal, 56*(3), 782–804.

Nylén, D., & Holmström, J. (2015). Digital innovation strategy: A framework for diagnosing and improving digital product and service innovation. *Business Horizons, 58*(1), 57–67.

OECD. (2005). Oslo Manual. *Guidelines for collecting and interpreting innovation data.* Paris: OECD Publication. Retrieved from http://www.sourceoecd.org/scienceIT/9264013083

Okon-Horodynska, E., Zachorowska-Mazurkiewicz, A., Wisla, R., & Sierotowicz, T. (2016). Gender, innovative capacity, and the process of innovation: A case of Poland. *Economics & Sociology, 9*(1), 252.

Østergaard, C. R., Timmermans, B., & Kristinsson, K. (2011). Does a different view create something new? The effect of employee diversity on innovation. *Research Policy*, *40*(3), 500–509.

Ozgen, C., Nijkamp, P., & Poot, J. (2013). The impact of cultural diversity on firm innovation: Evidence from Dutch micro-data. *IZA Journal of Migration*, *2*(1), 18.

Ozgen, C., Nijkamp, P., & Poot, J. (2017). The elusive effects of workplace diversity on innovation. *Papers in Regional Science*, *96*, S29–S49.

Randhawa, J. S., & Sethi, A. S. (2017). An empirical study to examine the role smart manufacturing in improving productivity and accelerating innovation. *International Journal of Engineering and Management Research (IJEMR)*, *7*(3), 607–615.

Schallmo, D., Williams, C. A., & Boardman, L. (2017). Digital transformation of business models—Best practice, enablers, and roadmap. *International Journal of Innovation Management*, *21*(08), 1740014.

Schrettle, S. (2013). Managing manufacturing process innovation? New manufacturing technology adoption as a dynamic capability. *University of St. Gallen*.

Shafie, S. Bin, Siti-Nabiha, A. K., & Tan, C. L. (2014). Organizational culture, transformational leadership and product innovation: A conceptual review. *International Journal of Organizational Innovation*, *7*.

Stamler, W. P., & Hannon, J. C. (2016). *Closing the innovation gap for business sustainability*. Walden University, Ann Arbor. Retrieved from https://search.proquest.com/docview/1799283712?accountid=30552

Thoben, K.-D., Wiesner, S., & Wuest, T. (2017). Industrie 4.0" and smart manufacturing – A review of research issues and application examples. *International Journal of Automotive Technology*, *11*(1).

Tseng, M.-L., Tan, R. R., & Siriban-Manalang, A. B. (2013). Sustainable consumption and production for Asia: Sustainability through green design and practice. *Journal of Cleaner Production*, *40*, 1–5.

van Acker, W., Wynen, J., & Op de Beeck, S. (2017). Illuminating the gender divide in public sector innovation: Evidence from the Australian Public Service. *Public Personnel Management*, *47*(2), 175–194. https://doi.org/10.1177/0091026017747299

Von Krogh, G., Netland, T., & Wörter, M. (2018). Winning with open process innovation. *MIT Sloan Management Review*, *59*(2), 53–56.

Wang, B. (2018). The future of manufacturing: A new perspective. *Engineering*.

Yamamoto, Y., & Bellgran, M. (2013). Four types of manufacturing process innovation and their managerial concerns. *Procedia CIRP*, *7*, 479–484.

Young, C., & Ghoshal, S. (2016). Organization theory and the multinational corporation. Springer.

Index

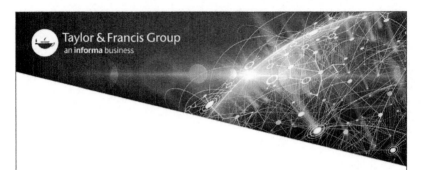

Printed in Great Britain
by Amazon

83331807R00066

ISBN 9780993487095

9 780993 487095

Originally published as a collection of ten short stories, Steaming into the North West has been developed to include a further ten tales from the rails.

Now taking us back to the very early days of steam, in the 1800s, these stories about life on the great Premier Line provide an entertaining and often thought-provoking insight into the tough, physical work that being an engineman entailed.

With early engines having no cab to speak of, life on the rails was open to all the elements. Danger came readily, from signalmen not paying attention to travelling through long, polluted tunnels.

Nevertheless, work on the railways was something to be proud of and, as with all the books in Michael Clutterbuck's Steaming into series, this is clearly portrayed through the cast of characters, attention to detail, and more than a little humour.